Nicholas Patrick Wiseman

The Hidden Gem.

A Drama in two Acts

Nicholas Patrick Wiseman

The Hidden Gem.
A Drama in two Acts

ISBN/EAN: 9783337304072

Printed in Europe, USA, Canada, Australia, Japan

Cover: Foto ©Thomas Meinert / pixelio.de

More available books at **www.hansebooks.com**

"THE HIDDEN GEM."

A

DRAMA IN TWO ACTS,

COMPOSED FOR THE COLLEGE JUBILEE

OF

ST. CUTHBERT'S, USHAW, 1858,

BY

H. E. CARDINAL WISEMAN.

WITH A PRELIMINARY ACCOUNT OF THE CELEBRATION

OF THE

COLLEGE JUBILEE.

LONDON:
THOMAS RICHARDSON AND SON, 147, STRAND;
9, CAPEL STREET, DUBLIN; AND DERBY.
MDCCCLIX.

TO THE

RT. REV. MONSIGNOR NEWSHAM, D.D.,

PRESIDENT OF ST. CUTHBERT'S COLLEGE,

MY TUTOR IN BOYHOOD,

MY PROFESSOR IN YOUTH,

AND

MY FRIEND THROUGH LIFE,

I AFFECTIONATELY AND REVERENTLY
DEDICATE THIS LITTLE WORK.

N. C. W.

NOTICE TO THE READER.

The Author of the following Drama having been obliged to leave London for a distant part of Europe, before the sheets of the "Preliminary Account" could be submitted to him, is not to be held responsible for such minute errors as may possibly have crept into that portion of the Work, since the Manuscript was sent by him to press.

THE EDITOR.

London, 9th Dec. 1859.

PRELIMINARY ACCOUNT

OF

ST. CUTHBERT'S COLLEGE

AND ITS

JUBILEE.

PRELIMINARY ACCOUNT

OF THE

JUBILEE OF ST. CUTHBERT'S COLLEGE.

The publication of a drama, composed expressly for the great Jubilee of St. Cuthbert's College, in the year 1858, has been felt by many attached friends and devoted *alumni* of that Community, to be a suitable occasion for placing on record the main facts of the celebration itself, prefaced by a brief sketch of the origin and earliest annals of the College, whose first era it brought to a close with such signal distinction. Such a notice, even although, far from rising to the rank of a chronicle, it were to shrink within the limits of a mere memorandum, would seem at any rate called for as a satisfaction to the filial instincts of so many loyal and loving hearts, no less than as a public tribute of gratitude to the venerable President and other superiors of St. Cuthbert's, tendered in the name of all those who, upon the occasion in question, were the recipients of their munificent hospitality, and the sharers of their festive joy.

Yet the difficulty which the historian attributes to the Athenian orator, is eminently and unaffectedly that of one who addresses himself to such a task. "Hard is it to praise where the language of eulogy must needs be felt by some to be in arrear of their forward sympathies, by others in advance of their tardy judgments."* So he who writes at once for the chivalrous sons of Ushaw, and for the colder-hearted critics of the world at large, finds it hard, indeed, to devise a form of phrase so nicely adjusted as to meet the expectations of readers so variously disposed, and to be chargeable neither by the one class with the error of defect, nor by the other with that of exaggeration. The only solution of the problem which occurs to the mind of the present writer, is to aim, as far as possible, at producing a narrative of facts, so simple as to risk the imputation rather of crudeness than of hyperbole, yet so faithful as to be open to no material correction from those who are qualified to pronounce upon it.

There is yet another reason, more publicly important than either of those already assigned, for giving some formal expression to the memory of the Ushaw Jubilee, while yet fresh and vigorous. That Jubilee is beyond question a great fact in our contemporaneous Catholic history; great in itself; great in its contrasts with the past; great in its auguries of the

---

* Vid. Thucyd. L. ii. c. 35.

future. In the second and third of these aspects it was the theme of eloquent description in the hands of more than one practised orator at its actual celebration. In the first, it was in itself more eloquent than any panegyric. It is no embellishment of the truth, but the bare truth itself, to note, that, within the precincts of a college devoted to the maintenance and teaching of the Catholic Faith in a country where that Faith, no such long time ago, was the object of wearing persecution, and is still the topic of a deep-rooted and extensive prejudice, there were gathered not scores, but hundreds, of the Catholic clergy and laity of Great Britain, and this, too, without the necessity of removing a single student from the immediate range of college discipline, as well as without the loss of necessary pastoral supervision to a single mission throughout the country. It is no exaggeration, but a simple fact, that in this great gathering was represented—yet no more than represented—not merely each element in Catholic society, and each function of our renewed ecclesiastical constitution, but those elements and functions especially whose very presence in the midst of us is a token of the restoration of Catholic order, and the reproduction of Catholic life, such as no superciliousness can ignore and no prejudice can blink. For not merely were there prelates of England, who, though but a fraction of our hierarchy, outnumbered the full complement of our bishops in times within the memory of the younger amongst us,* and the representatives of capitular bodies, who evidence, not the establishment only, but the consolidation, of that hierarchy which was met, upon its introduction, by so much of open resistance, and so much of sinister prediction; but chiefly **were** there to be seen in large numbers the more recent **converts** to our Faith, bearing upon their features that inimitable expression of peace, and in their gait that incommunicable air of happy freedom and confidence, which can come of nothing but the consciousness of security. Surely all this was enough to stamp the celebration with importance, and **invest it** with interest. Had it, indeed, been **the** object of some painter, or some dramatic mechanist, to group **in** striking combination, or bring out in vivid prominence, the various facts **and** characters of our latest history, not so much **in** their aggregate, as by representation and specimen, he could hardly have produced a more successful result of his art or contrivance than was the unstudied and unsought effect of this free action and fortuitous concurrence.

Yet it is certain that, to **estimate the** full importance of the event, we must take it in connection with the earlier antecedents of St. Cuthbert's College,

---

* There were but four Vicars Apostolic in England before the year 1840.

and with the circumstances from which that College derived its beginning. Hence, any notice of the Jubilee of 1858 would be essentially imperfect which did not touch, at least, upon the history of Ushaw College, and of the Church in England, so far as it bears upon Ushaw.

It is well known that, previously to the breaking out of the Great French Revolution, the priests, who kept alive the flickering embers of our holy religion in England, received their ecclesiastical education in great numbers at the English College of Douai, then **conducted** by Secular Clergy. The progress of **that** terrible Revolution, as the nature of its aims, and the character of its agents, were more and more plainly developed, naturally became a subject of the utmost alarm to the inmates of ecclesiastical seminaries, and especially to such as, like those of Douai and St. Omer, were the nurseries of the English clergy. Some time **before** the storm burst in all its fury upon the English College at Douai, the menace of its approach had the effect of driving **many** of the students to **their** native country. It **was** as early as the beginning of the year 1793 that they began to arrive in England. There being, at that time, no place of ecclesiastical education for Catholics in this country, these young men had no resource but to return to their friends. At length the Right Rev. Dr. Douglass, **then** Vicar Apostolic of the London District, acting in conjunction with Dr. Gibson, Vicar Apostolic of the Northern District, and fearing the effect of this interruption of ecclesiastical studies, and yet more the moral consequences of a transition from a life of wholesome discipline to one of indolence and relaxation, summoned these students from their homes, and placed them under the care of the Reverend Mr. Potier, who kept a lay school at Old Hall Green, in Hertfordshire, where many of the scattered students were thus assembled before the end of the year 1793. These students numbered nearly twenty, so that it became necessary to make alterations in Mr. Potier's house with a view to their reception.

About a month before this arrangement was carried into effect, the storm of revolutionary fury, which had been so long expected, fell with tremendous violence upon the English College at Douai. President, professors, and students, to the number of forty-one, were hurried off to the citadel of Doulens, and there imprisoned. This occurred on the 16th of October. On the 24th of the next month four of this party made their escape, and on the 15th of the January following (1794) eleven more succeeded in leaving the fortress, by means of a rope let down from the walls. By the great mercy of Providence aiding their own heroic spirit of enterprise, the whole fifteen effected a safe landing in

England, though not till after many difficulties and dangers. A portion of the eleven, whose escape was the later, on their arrival in London, repaired to the house of Dr. Douglass, the Vicar Apostolic. Whether from the difficulty of finding accommodation for them in the over-crowded establishment of Mr. Potier in Hertfordshire, or from some other unexplained cause, his Lordship made no suggestions to them about repairing to Old Hall Green. They had no option, therefore, but to betake themselves to their homes, which lay in the north of England. Here they soon came under the eye of Dr. Gibson, the Vicar Apostolic of the Northern District, and were sent by his Lordship to a lay-school kept by the Rev. Arthur Storey, at Tudhoe, near Durham. The first to avail himself of the Bishop's kindness was Mr. (afterwards the Reverend) Thomas Cock, who arrived at Tudhoe on the 10th of March, 1794. He was soon joined by Messrs. Rickaby, Dawson, and Storey. And here our brief historical survey brings us to a name not only dear to the sons of St. Cuthbert's, but intimately and honourably connected with the literature of our country. Among those who had received their education at Douai, was the justly celebrated Dr. Lingard, at that time tutor in the family of Lord Stourton. On hearing that some of his former pupils had arrived at Tudhoe, he requested, and obtained, **leave to join** them, and once more became their teacher.

Among **the** Douai students, who had previously been placed **by** Dr. Douglass at Old Hall Green, some were subjects of the Northern District. Desirous of removing to the scene of their future labours, these students made application **to Dr. Gibson to** receive them. **But** the difficulty **was to find a** place suitable **for an** ecclesiastical college, **since, as we** have already said, the establishment at **Tudhoe was** purely secular. By **one of** those remarkable **coincidences** which so clearly **denote** the hand of Divine Providence in the whole of this memorable passage of **our** ecclesiastical history, Dr. Gibson happened, when he received the application **of the Old** Hall Green students, to be **on a visi**t at the **house** of Mr. Silvertop, **who** was able to assist him **in his difficulty.**

The Bishop resolved, as a preliminary step, **upon** removing **his** students from Tudhoe to Pontop Hall. Pontop Hall was the seat of a Catholic mission, the duties of which were discharged by **the** Reverend Thomas Eyre, who resided about two miles distant from Crook Hall, which was **a** deserted mansion of the Baker family, situated near Lanchester, in the county of Durham. To Pontop Hall, accordingly, the students collected at Tudhoe at once repaired under the conduct of Dr. Lingard, and took up their residence in Mr. **Eyre's mission-house.** This occurred on the 9th of September, 1794. Here the students from Tudhoe were soon joined by Messrs. Bradley and Lupton.

On the 15th of the following October, the house at Crook was in a condition to receive the new colony, which on that day was finally located in it. The 15th of October, 1794, is therefore the date of the foundation of the first ecclesiastical college of the Northern District, and that which was the nursery of the future St. Cuthbert's.

Critics, far severer than any to whose eye these pages are likely to be subjected, will surely excuse, even if they cannot appreciate, the minute, the almost punctilious precision with which dates, apparently trivial, and names, which, however justly dear to those who remember them, and however precious for the inappreciable services of those who bore them, are, (with one great and other lesser exceptions) comparatively unknown to the world at large, have here, of set purpose and with full deliberation, been brought under public review. We are now recounting, (it must be borne in mind), however imperfectly, the steps, few, yet momentous, silent, yet sure, by which these our pilgrim-fathers, exiles and wayfarers from their youth up, and heroes in God's army before their youth's close, are wending their way by the light of faith and obedience to their destined but as yet unrevealed home; thence, again, after a brief sojourn, to come forth with energy recruited, and strong in holy lore, that they may sow the seeds of that great harvest of which **we, their** successors, **are now** reaping the fruits. **It may be** permitted us, therefore, **with** reverent and loving exactitude, to note their progress, and treat their memory with somewhat **of** that religious regard wherewith the ancient Romans preserved the foot-prints and enshrined **the** names of the **founders of** their race.

The new college at Crook Hall was placed by **the** Bishop under the presidency of the Reverend Thomas Eyre, who was removed from the Pontop Mission to take charge of it. At the same time Dr. Lingard became Vice-President. Mr. John Bell, who had been engaged as tutor in the Silvertop family, was called upon by the Bishop **to** fill the office of General Prefect. These gentlemen constituted the professorial staff of the college, and began their work with the forementioned refugee students, to whom was added, in the following month, Mr. Henry Silvertop, the late Mr. Witham of Lartington, who had quitted Douai on the first outbreak of the revolution.

As **soon as the** college at Crook Hall came into active operation, Dr. Gibson requested Dr. Douglass to send **to** it from Old Hall Green such of the students as belonged to the Northern District. These were six in number: their names were, Charles Saul, Edward Monk, Richard Thompson, Thomas Gillow,

Thomas **Penswick**, and George **Lee** Haydock. These, with the exception of the last named, repaired to Crook Hall at once, and arrived there before **the end** of the year **1794.** Mr. Eyre, the President, who **had** himself **filled** many important offices **at** Douai, proceeded to model the new college precisely upon the type of his former Alma Mater, and to the present day the constitutions and regulations **of** Douai **College are** preserved **and carried** out in **St.** Cuthbert's College with scrupulous fidelity.

The English Secular College **at St.** Omer would **seem to** have suffered **by** the Revolution, even **more than the** sister institution of Douai. Few, comparatively, of its inmates had withdrawn from it before the arrival of the Republican troops, and the President, Dr. Gregory Stapleton, the Professors, and no less than sixty-four of the students, were seized and thrown into prison, first at Arras, and subsequently at Doulens, at both of which fortresses they suffered the most cruel hardships.

Upon the fall of Robespierre, the English prisoners were released, and such of them as had been members of the two colleges, arrived in England on the 2nd of March, 1795.

Of the twenty-six Professors and students **who** came with **the** Reverend John Daniel, the President **of Douai** College, **the** following **five** proceeded to

Crook Hall: Joseph Swinburne, John Penswick,* Matthew Forster, Robert Gradwell,† and Thomas Berry, while three of their number, John Delany, Richard Brodrick, and Lewis Havard, entered the academy of Mr. Potier, at Old Hall Green. This fresh accession to the numbers at Crook Hall, raised the complement of Professors and students, exclusively of the President, the Reverend Thomas Eyre, to twenty-one.

The number of students in Mr. Potier's academy, at Old Hall Green, was now increased by the addition of Dr. Stapleton, with one Professor and twelve students. The number of refugee students, was thirteen from St. Omer and nine from Douai, making in all twenty-two. About this time the establishment was removed from the care of Mr. Potier, and placed under that of Dr. Stapleton, who was formally installed by Dr. Douglass, as the first President of the College of Old Hall Green. This was on the Feast of the Assumption, 1795, which accordingly forms the date of the foundation of St. Edmund's College. The rules and constitutions of that college were not founded strictly upon the model either of Douai or St. Omer, although Dr. Stapleton

---

* The only priest now living, who studied at the old college of Douai.

† Afterwards coadjutor to the Vicar-Apostolic of the London District.

had **been** connected with both of those seminaries, **but were** selected from the codes of each, according to **Dr.** Stapleton's judgment of their suitableness to the occasion. It thus appears that Old Hall College, through its first President, who had been also President of St. Omer's, derives its origin from St. Omer's rather than from Douai, whereas the College of Ushaw is strictly and exclusively the lineal descendant of Douai.

Previously to this period, the bishops and leading clergy were actively engaged in the attempt to form one **great** Ecclesiastical Seminary for the whole of England, at Thorpe Arch, near Wetherby, in Yorkshire. The project, however, was relinquished about the month of June, 1795, whereupon the Reverend John Daniel, the President of Douai College, went, in company with **Dr.** Gibson, to Crook Hall, and was by his Lordship formally installed as President in the place of the Reverend Thomas Eyre, who resigned in his favour, and accepted the office of Vice-President. This arrangement **was** effected upon the Feast of SS. Peter and Paul. Before the close of the Octave, Dr. Stapleton, who had been President of the English College at St. Omer, and **who had** lately replaced Mr. Potier as head of the Academy at Old Hall Green arrived at Crook Hall, and after a long conference, the original arrangement was restored, **and Mr.** Eyre resumed the office of President. The bishop then took his leave, in company with Dr. Stapleton. The object of this purely amicable change was to enable Mr. Daniel to make his claim upon the French Government for the sequestrated property of Douai College, under the title of President of that College; a title which he retained till his death, at Paris, in the year 1823.

Dr. Gibson, who had never ceased to entertain the project of establishing **a large** College for the Northern District, since the plan of a general place of ecclesiastical education for England had been abandoned, and who founded the College at Crook Hall as the instalment of a far more important undertaking, had, by the year 1804, so far matured his plans, as to begin the **work** which was finally completed four years later. **The** spot chosen for the new College was Ushaw, near Durham.

At length, **on** the nineteenth day of July, 1808, the house **at** Crook Hall was evacuated, and its inmates took possession of their new and more commodious quarters. The transit from the one house to the other was made in a manner so simple as to be absolutely primitive and patriarchal. The Rev. Thomas Eyre, the President, "having first," (as is testified by an authentic record,) "carefully locked the door of each and every room" of the abandoned house, proceeded, on foot, accompanied by his professors and students, to the new house at Ushaw, distant **about** nine miles. The original College of **Ushaw** still remains, and **a** wish has been expressed, which will probably find an echo in many hearts, that this portion **of** the present building should **be** preserved with **an almost** religious care. However different **from** the splendid fabric which has grown up around and about it, it **has** an interest which the lapse of time, far from diminishing, **will** but increase in an accelerated ratio, both as the older building **throws** out, **in a kind** of relief, the **magni**tude of the work which has grown out **of it;** and, yet more, as it forms a standing memento of days, **the** retrospect of which must ever **be a** subject of intense gratitude to those who have **lived** to witness the progress of religion in England.

Just fifty years from the date of this singular exodus, and simple inauguration, upon how different a scene did the bright sun of July cast down its **cheer**ing rays! Its dawning light, indeed, disclosed **in** their garb of sober grey the **outline** of those gently sloping hills. **Its** parting beams flung **across** that varied landscape, the glowing tints of eve. **Old** Durham's sullen bell, less **the** herald of **a joyful** service, than the knell of a departed Sacrifice, chimed, or rather tolled, its summons, at morn, and eventide, to a church despoiled of its life, and a worship denuded of its poetry. These were the same; yet were there changes both material and moral. The miracles of one era had become the customary facts of another. Time had been economized, labour epitomized, space all but annihilated. Travelling, then a toil, was now a luxury, and priests were sped, or rather spirited, through the yielding air, from London to York, in hardly a longer time than that score of holy adventurers had taken to plod their tedious way from Crook to Ushaw.

Yet of all the marvels which that half century had wrought, none, perhaps, was greater than the marvel of St. Cuthbert's itself. A college, no unworthy compeer of the noblest of our mediæval institutions, had spread its goodly amplitude. A magnificent chapel, with its cluster of tributary oratories, a library, a museum of vast length, a refectory of stately proportions, a spacious theatre of literary exhibition, ample rooms, lines of dormitories, and almost a mileage of cloister, had sprung up, as if by miracle. But we are lingering at the starting-point of our work, though, as we fear, we have almost exhausted the reader's patience. Let us proceed, then, at once to the Jubilee.

It will not be expected that, in recording the event of this memorable celebration, we should attempt in a necessarily brief and preliminary notice, to set down more than the leading facts, or draw attention to other features of the occasion than those by which it was distinguished from ordinary college festivals. Hence we must pass over very cursorily the proceedings of the first and third of the three days devoted to the commemoration, for it was the second of those days which impressed a peculiar character upon the occasion. But here an exception must be made in favour of an incident which, though it occurred on one of those less prominent days, was entirely characteristic of the Jubilee itself—the inauguration of the "Jubilee Fund," for the advancement of objects connected with the educational interests of the College. For a similar reason, many addresses delivered on the occasion must be omitted, and others materially curtailed. And we must dismiss in a single sentence such features of the occasion as the splendours of the hospitality, the kindness with which it was dispensed, the enthusiasm of the students, the credit reflected by them in various ways upon the care of which they are unceasingly the objects, and the good feeling and happy cheerfulness which prevailed far and wide throughout the immense assemblage of visitors. Indeed, the invitation by which the eye of each new comer was met on his arrival at the door of the College, received on the part of all its marked and practical response.

SALVETE · HOSPITES

DIEM · AVSPICATISSIMVM · CONCELEBRATVRI

ESTO · PROCVL · A · LIMINE · QVIDQVID · NOCET · VEL · ANGIT

QVIN · VOBIS · ADVENIENTIBVS · OCCVRRANT · PAX ·
ET · GAVDIVM

DIMIDIATVM · SAECVLVM · QVAE ·
SIGNAT · LVX

DET · FELICEM · ANNIS · ANTEACTIS · EXITVM

LAETVM · VENTVRIS · OMEN

QVARE · ET · VOS · **DOMVM** · INTRANTES · OMNIA
FAVSTA · ADPRECAMINI

ET · VNA · MENTE · ATQVE · VOCE · CONCLAMATE

HAVETE · VOS.

The Jubilee day, Wednesday, the 21st July, 1858, was opened by the offering of the Adorable Sacrifice, with its more solemn and festive accompaniments, in the magnificent chapel of the College, after many private celebrations **of** the numerous bishops and priests collected in the house. The High Mass was celebrated by the Right Reverend Dr. Hogarth, Bishop of Hexham, in the presence of the Cardinal Archbishop of the Province. There were present, in episcopal habit, besides the celebrant and assisting

Cardinal, the following bishops of England and Scotland; the Right Rev. Dr. Briggs, Bishop of **Beverley**; the Right Reverend Dr. Gillis, **Bishop** of Limyra, and Vicar Apostolic of the Eastern District of Scotland; the Right Reverend Dr. Roskell, Bishop of Nottingham; the Hon. and Right Reverend Dr. Clifford, Bishop of Clifton; and the Right Reverend Dr. Amherst, Bishop of Northampton. The following prelates were also present; **the** Hon. and Right Reverend Monsignor Talbot, Chamberlain **to** His Holiness; the Right Reverend Monsignor Weedall, D.D.; and the Right Reverend Monsignor Newsham, **D.D.** With these were united in assistance at the holy solemnities, a vast concourse of clergy and laity, whose names it would be impossible, consistently with our present limits, to particularize.

The sermon was preached **by** the Cardinal Archbishop, from the text, **Lev. xxv.** 10, "They shall sanctify the fiftieth year; for it is the year of Jubilee." **A** few extracts from **this** discourse, taken from the notes of a short-hand writer present at it, are necessary to the completeness of the present notice.

The Cardinal began by observing that Time is the gift of God; and that there is no portion of it, whether small or large, but must have its festival. The Church, however, counts not by weeks, or months, or years alone, but must commemorate all those greater divisions of time which denote her progress towards her consummation. All who take the law of God for their rule, and the practice of the Church for their model, must desire to mark those epochs which are sanctified under both Dispensations, by corresponding celebrations. St. Cuthbert's College has thus reached a point in its history at which it does well to plant a land-mark, which may be seen at a distance, and become sacred to those who follow us, and which may, above all, be revered and honoured as a monument of Divine Goodness. It is right that such a Jubilee should be celebrated, and celebrated as becomes those who believe that whatever of prosperity, of happiness, or of joy descends upon us is the gift of God. It is in this spirit that the day of our festivity is begun by a solemn offering of the first-fruits to God..

The day from which St. Cuthbert's dates its beginning is so clearly defined, and its characteristics so strongly marked, that it never can be repeated. That day was once, and is for ever gone, like the day of a man's birth. It cannot recur. But how shall we make this day other than the hundreds and thousands which have preceded it, or may follow it? If we approach a stream which is for ever flowing, and watch its course for a time, and then leave it and return to it after an interval, it seems to us the same. Every ripple, every little wave which we had noticed, murmurs over the pebbles; every hollow which it makes round the stones that for a moment arrest its course; every sweeping rush around a projecting point, every deep calm pool beneath the overshadowing tree—all is the same. And yet, while we are looking on, not a drop, not a particle, of that water remains for an instant in its place. While we have been watching these movements, all has flowed on and beyond us, never, never, to return. It is so with the history of this House. It is at once liable to a perpetual change, yet possesses an endless stability.

"Some of you," said the preacher, "will return here after a longer or a shorter interval, and it will appear to you precisely the same. You will see the same professors, the same pupils, almost the same countenances repeated in every gradation, from the child to the man's. There are the same friendly sounds, the same studies, the same duties, the same unvarying round of observances. And yet, not one particle of this whole but is in constant flux. The child of to-day is the boy of to-morrow—and so of others. Thus, while the whole order and operation of things remain untouched, yet in a few years not one of these atoms will remain."

The preacher then proceeded to say that it became necessary to mark the great day on which they had met, by some extraordinary token. Such a token was found in the sacred relic, which it was proposed then solemnly to inaugurate, and thus render the day memorable indeed in the annals of the college. That day, then, was to be placed, under the custody of St. Cuthbert's Church and St. Cuthbert's College, the ring borne by the saint, under whose patronage they lived. He then went on to trace the history of this precious relic.

"It is perfectly certain," said the Cardinal, "that, when the **tomb** of St. Cuthbert was opened by the Royal Commissioners in 1537,—concerning the identity of which tomb at its first opening no doubt has ever existed,—there **was found** upon the finger **of the saint,** his episcopal ring of **gold,** with sapphire stones of great **beauty.** It passed into the keeping of the last Catholic Dean, afterwards Bishop, of Durham, Thomas Watson. From him it passed, through another hand, into the possession of Lord Montague, who sheltered **in his** house, besides other priests, the **Rev.** Richard Smith, **first Vicar** Apostolic **of** England. He, **yielding to** the pressure **of the** times, retired abroad, and died in a religious house **in** Paris, which he had founded on the rule of **St.** Augustine. **To the members of** that community he left this precious **relic which has remained with them up** to the time **of** its transmission here. **Never for a** moment, even **during** the terrible French Revolution, **during which** that single religious house was spared, did this relic pass from the keeping of its holy guardians, or from the shrine, poor indeed, in which it was contained. If any **one** asked **those** religious what value they set **upon this precious** object, **they** would answer, as I have heard them answer, **that it bore to them** a double value ; first, as it was a **sacred memorial of one** of the saints of the **ancient** English Church, and secondly, as a legacy of their pious **founder.** Again, and again, on **my** visiting Paris and that **house,** the relic was brought to me **to** venerate. It seemed **to** strike the religious, that I had some feeling upon the subject. **Once,** at length, it was **said to** me, 'You think **this** relic ought to be in England.' 'Certainly,' I replied : 'I think the relics of every English saint find their natural home in England.' 'Why?' 'Because you will remember, that, when Jerusalem was besieged, and the time of its doom had come, as the signal that God had given it up to vengeance, and would not be reconciled to this favoured city, a voice was heard, saying that the saints were departing from it. And so, the doom of this country was sealed, when the saints, who had been removed in spirit, were removed also in body...... What brighter sign can there be, that the time of reconciliation is at hand, than that the saints who once departed are returning to 'us?' The next time I visited the House, little thinking of the consolation which awaited me, but having said that one thing only was wanted to make St. Cuthbert's College, truly St. Cuthbert's own—this pledge of his presence—it was whispered in my ear, 'If you will ask for St. Cuthbert's ring, for St. Cuthbert's College, it will be granted you.' Instantly I made the application; and, by an act of self-denial and self-sacrifice, which I call heroic, those Religious sent back the ring, and this day I wear it; the first time that a bishop of the Catholic Church has borne it on his finger. And you shall be the witnesses of its authentication and enshrinement, and venerate it with the encouragement which I am happy to announce, has been awarded by the Holy Father, of a Plenary Indulgence. I will not enter upon the question whether the ring were actually worn by the Saint during his life, or whether it were put with other things upon his body when the tomb was opened about the year 1100. Suffice it for us, that it has been borne on that sacred hand for hundreds of years."

At the end of Mass the whole of the bishops assisting, signed the formal document of authentication. The ring was then venerated; each of the persons present coming up to the sanctuary where the Cardinal Archbishop stood, wearing the ring which was kissed by all in succession.

At the appointed hour the company assembled in the hall of exhibition. The gradual gathering of the

vast assembly into this magnificent apartment, the incidents attending upon **it, and the** spectacle exhibited, are thus described by an eye-witness, recording his impressions when they were still fresh and vivid.

"The exhibition-room at Ushaw is one of the most splendid apartments **of that** splendid house......It **is** of majestic height and **ample** dimensions. At the **end** are tiers of seats rising to more than half the height of the room, **and opposite, on** occasion of the Jubilee, was a stage, tastefully and judiciously arranged for the purpose, whether of an orchestra or a theatre. In the centre of the front row of the rising tier sat the Cardinal Archbishop, with bishops and prelates ranging on either side of him to the right and left......We could wish that **this** scene had been photographed. The dress worn by the bishops and prelates on such semi-state occasions **is one** of the most graceful and **beautiful that can** be imagined. **It** brought them **out in** strong relief to **the** rest of the assemblage, who **were** in ordinary costume, and as most were clergy, the contrast **was the more** striking. The absence of study **and** formality greatly added to the effect of the scene. Behind the bishops and other visitors rose in ascending gradation the ranks of enthusiastic students. But we are anticipating matters. The line **of** dignitaries is not **yet** filled. The last of the visitors is in **the** hall; in the gallery hosts of impatient youths, on the floor knots of priests and laymen busily engaged in conversation. Suddenly there is a cheer which almost appals you............Again a brief interval, and then another cheer as stunning as the former. A seat at the Cardinal's right hand has been filled, but its venerable occupant has taken possession of it almost like an apparition. So modestly, so noiselessly, so unobservedly did he glide to it, that you are fain to doubt whence and how he came, though the cheer which has startled you is proof positive that a hundred eyes descried his approach, and a hundred hearts were strung up to the cracking point to peal forth his welcome. Another, and another, and another cheer! It is for the patriarch among our bishops, the Bishop of Beverley, whose singularly beautiful and venerable appearance must secure him attention in any assembly, and whose benevolent eye, beaming with the light of kindness, and the promise of " play-days," especially endears him to the sympathies of studious youth. Or that cheer speaks to strangers of the affection borne to the venerable Bishop of Hexham, well-loved because well-known, or of the popularity of Scotland's gifted prelate, and Ushaw's adopted son, the amiable and eloquent Gillis."*

The proceedings of the day were opened with an address spoke by Mr. Arthur Wilberforce, a promising scion of that distinguished family, and the grandson of the eminent English philanthropist, whose distinguished career was coeval with the primitive, and, as we may call them, primo-primitive, annals of Ushaw College.

This address was followed by five congratulatory orations delivered in succession by the following gentlemen; the Honourable Charles Langdale; the Very Reverend Dr. Russell, President of St. Patrick's College, Maynooth; Sir William Lawson, Baronet; the Very Reverend Frederick Oakeley, Canon, and the Very Reverend Henry Edward Manning, Provost, of the Metropolitan Chapter of Westminster. Mr. Langdale, with the manly and forcible eloquence characteristic of himself, and so full of that " moral persuasiveness," which is the greatest charm of

* Dublin Review, Oct. 1858.

oratory, took a retrospect of the "last fifty years" of St. Cuthbert's. Dr. Russell followed, upon the subject of Dr. Lingard's eminent services to historical literature. Sir William Lawson gave a most interesting sketch of the benefits conferred by Ushaw upon the Church in England. Canon Oakeley made an address upon "Catholic Collegiate Education," especially in its religious aspect, illustrated by his experience of Oxford,* and the Provost of Westminster wound up the series by an eloquent anticipation of the probable course of events in Catholic England during the period of which the Jubilee, in bringing the last half century to a close, formed the beginning.

The Cardinal Archbishop, having summed up the argument of these several addresses, the proceedings ended with the performance of the following

JUBILEE ODE.

I.

No breezes play, no sunbeams smile,
Throughout the length of Britain's isle,
Upon a more loved honoured pile
    Than this our College home;
Heir of the rays, which no more shine
In Finchale's vale, on banks of Tyne,
Round holy Cuthbert's rifled shrine,
    Or Bede's yet hallowed tomb.

---

* This Address, of which a written copy had been preserved, is just published uniformly with the present work.

CHORUS.

Then join in chorus, man and boy,
   Long reign in this our noble College
   Celestial truth and earthly knowledge,
Study's toil, and virtue's joy.

II.

We love our church, its image, stalls,
Our graceful chapels, noble halls,
Our ambulacra's pictured walls,
     Our library's rich lore.
We love our ball-place, lake, and bounds,
Our merry games' perennial rounds,
The hubbub of their joyful sounds,
     Shouts, cheers, and laughter's roar.

CHORUS.

Then join in chorus, man and boy,
   Long reign in this our noble College
   Celestial truth and earthly knowledge,
Study's toil, and virtue's joy.

III.

But hush! good spirits fill the air:
They come our joy and love to share,
Great Lingard, Gibson, Gillow, Eyre,
     Who sleep beneath our sod;
And many a one, whose youthful head
Soon drooped above the tainted bed,
Then sank among the martyred dead:
     The path here taught who trod.

CHORUS.

Then join in chorus, man and boy,
   Long reign in this our noble College
   Celestial truth with earthly knowledge,
Study's toil, and virtue's joy.

IV.

Then up, up, cheerily, dash we on!
Not words, but deeds, mark Ushaw's son!
The world's wide battle field upon,
    With evil deadly strife!
In faith uncompromising zeal,
Devotion to our country's weal,
Charity, honour, virtue—seal,
    Brothers! our coming life.

CHORUS.

Then join in chorus, man and boy,
    Long reign in this our noble College
    Celestial truth and earthly knowledge,
Study's toil, and virtue's joy.

After the Jubilee Banquet, rendered chiefly remarkable by the enthusiastic reception of a speech from the Right Reverend Monsignor Talbot, in reply to the proposal of the Health of Pope Pius IX., the company assembled once more in the Hall of Exhibition to witness the representation of the Drama which has given rise to this preliminary sketch. And having brought our historical record to this point, we will close it with one observation. If on an occasion when there were so many subjects to awaken interest, and so many names to elicit enthusiasm, it be possible to select one subject and one name above the rest, as those which were uppermost in the minds, and nearest to the lips, of this great company, they were those which are commemorated in the following lines, the recital of which was hailed by the audience as the opportunity of displaying their feelings in one last, united, and long-continued burst of thrilling acclamation. Those lines will form the appropriate close of the present sketch.

> *Carinus.* But surely few could measure back that term
>   Of half a century?
> *Alexius.*   Alas! but few.
>   And in the house one only. In the midst
>   Of all he sate, uniting old and young,
>   Friends of his youth, disciples of his age;
>   So that he smiled on all, and made all smile.
>   His life the chain, which, threading one by one
>   The circlets of past fifty years, joined them
>   Into one generation. Many hung
>   From ring or link; alone he held both ends.
>   So many had he led on wisdom's path,
>   So many had sustained up virtue's steep,
>   That by consent they called him all—" THE DOCTOR,"
>   Aye, " THE OLD DOCTOR" was their name of love.

PROLOGUE

TO "THE HIDDEN GEM."

Recited at the performance of that drama by the *members of the Catholic Institute of St.* **Philip Neri,** *at Liverpool, on the 26th of January,* 1859.

Unscar'd by menace, unreform'd by age,
Deaf to the voice of prophet, priest, and sage,
Despite Experience's instructive rules,
The pith of proverbs, and the lore of schools,
Which tell, in words of wisdom from of old,
How all that glitters is not therefore gold;
The knowing world, in changeless accents cries,
" The gold that glitters is the gold *I* prize."
  Yet might the world its eye sagacious turn
To Nature's truthful tablets, there to learn
The ways and workings of mysterious Grace,
In type reflected on Creation's face;
Sure it had known how precious things of earth
On hearts unthankful waste their useless worth;

How gifts of goodliest form and fairest bloom
Lurk in the deep, or slumber in the gloom;
How caves unfathom'd hide the priceless ore,
And pearls of ocean strew the desert shore,
And sweetest flowers of summer live and die,
Unseen, unheeded, save by Angel's eye:
Taught by these monitors, the world might know
How purest treasure oft may poorest show.

O, knew we but our bliss, the happiest we,
To whom 'tis giv'n this gracious truth to see,
Not couch'd in emblem, nor **by** hint convey'd,
But in the Church**'s book to** Faith display'd!
For sure the Church is that prolific Field,
Whose depths unsearch'd no answ'ring produce yield;
She is that Garden, where **the** gifts of Spring
On arid winds their fruitless fragrance fling;
The Casket she, where gems unnotic'd lie,
The staple of Heav'n**'s** beauteous jewelry.

A gem **like this, so** hidden, yet so bright,
We set **before** you, Christian friends, to night.
The young Alexius, rich and nobly **born,**
Gave all to God; then, "lonely, **not** forlorn,"
By men despis'd, but full of heav'nly joy,
He roam'd from place to **place, a** pilgrim boy;
Then, sped by holy warnings back to Rome,
He lived **a** stranger in his childhood's home;

And, worthiest he the son's award to share,
Chose the slave's part, and priz'd the menial's fare;
Till, in Affliction's furnace tried and prov'd,
Spurn'd where he trusted, slighted where he lov'd,
He laid him down and died.   But Truth hath said,
" The corn of wheat first liveth, when 'tis dead;"*
So he, I ween, did pass through bitter strife,
From living death to bright undying life.

Saint Philip's children, in Saint Philip's name,
Not your applause, but your indulgence claim;
Fain would they proffer, in this simple Play,
Saint Philip's truth in his own child-like way.
Yet, might your genial smile once beam on them,
This Tale itself might prove "a hidden gem,"
In flowers illusive wrapt.   For not alone
The moor's drear vastness, or the desert's stone,
O'erlays the mine which teems with embryo wealth,
Or hides the fount whence issue streams of health;
The ore may sleep beneath the garden's crest,
The blue waves laugh† around the jewel's nest,
And woods of em'rald foliage lure the eye
To where deep springs of health embedded lie.‡

* St. John xii. 24, 25.

† ανήριθμον γέλασμα πόντου,—*Æschyl.*

‡ It is often remarked that mineral springs are found in the midst of romantic scenery.

And thou, dear Prince, in loving presence here,*
Our toil to lighten, and our hearts to cheer;
Wont from the care of Churches to descend,
At pray'r of children, or at suit of friend,
If haply, like Saint Philip, thou may'st win
Some wayward soul from error, or from sin;
Thou art the pole-star of our course to-night;
If thou be near, the low'ring sky grows bright;
What frown shall scare us, if we feel *thy* love?
What critic dare to blame, if *thou* approve?

F. Can. O.

---

* The writer feels it necessary to observe, in explanation, that His Eminence, Cardinal Wiseman, was present on the occasion for which this Prologue was written.

THE ARGUMENT.

In the reign of the Emperor Honorius and the Pontificate of Innocent I., there lived on the Aventine, a Roman Patrician of great wealth, named Euphemianus. He had an only son, Alexius, whom he educated in principles of solid piety, and in the practice of unbounded charity. When he was grown up, but still young, a Divine command ordered the son to quit his father's house, and lead the life of a poor pilgrim. He accordingly repaired to Edessa, where he lived several years, while he was sought for in vain over all the world. At length he was similarly ordered to return home; and was received as a stranger into his father's house.

He remained there as many years as he had lived abroad, amidst the scorn and ill-treatment of his own domestics, until his death: when first a voice, heard through all the churches in the city, proclaimed him a Saint, and then a paper, written by himself, revealed his history.

As the years passed by Alexius in these two conditions have been variously stated by different writers, in this Drama they have been limited to five spent in each, or ten in all.

The beginning and the close of the second period, of that passed at home, form the subject of this composition; so that five years are supposed to elapse between its two acts.

Such is the domestic history, recorded in Rome, on the Aventine hill, where the beautiful church of St. Alexius yet stands, and is visited, on his feast, by crowds of his fellow-citizens. The view from its garden is one of the most charming in Rome. The basilica of Santa Sabina is next door to it.

DRAMATIS PERSONÆ.

Euphemianus, a Roman Patrician.
Alexius, under the name of *Ignotus*, his son.
Carinus, a boy, his nephew.
Proculus, his Freedman and Steward.
Eusebius, freed after Act i.
Bibulus,......................
Davus,......................... } Slaves.
Ursulus, } Black..........
Verna,
Gannio, a Beggar.
An Imperial Chamberlain.
An Officer.
Slaves, white and black.
Two Robbers.

Scene on the Aventine Hill in Rome, partly outside, partly in the court or Atrium, of Euphemian's house, in the Reign of Honorius, and the Pontificate of Innocent I.

"THE HIDDEN GEM."

ACT I.

Scene I.—*An open space on the Aventine, with houses on one side, and trees on the other. At the back is the door of Euphemian's house. Under the trees is a marble bench.*

Enter Alexius, *tired, wearing a cloak. Sits for a moment to rest, then rises.*

Alexius. Thus far I feel, that to the very letter
I have obeyed the clear commands of heaven.
"Where first thine eyes saw light, there must
    they close:
"Where first thy life began, there shall it end."—
Such were the words the voice mysterious spake.
So, longing to complete my pilgrimage,
Once more I stand, where haughty Aventine
Crushes, with craggy heel, the serpent neck
Of writhing Tiber; while, between the peaks
Of Sabine hills, the sun shoots forked beams,
Hanging the gems of morning on each leaf.

If Italy, **or Rome, or** Aventine
Was meant, my goal is reached—but oh, remains
   there
One step more, o'er that threshold—[*looking
   towards Euphemian's house*] there **to die**?
For **there** I first drew breath.—It cannot be.
Five **years it** is to-day, since I was sent,
Like him of Ur, from father's house and kindred.
What sorrow, perhaps worse, hath been endured
For me, within the compass of those walls!
Livest thou yet, sweet mother? Dost thou shake
Thy palsied **head and** quivering hand, in anguish,
O'er thy long-lost, but unforgotten child?
Or dost thou, from thy patiently won throne
Look down and smile, upon thy pilgrim son?—
I know my father lives; his name is written
Upon the dypticks of far distant churches,
As on men's hearts, **in** charity's gold letters.—
How can **I stand** before him? How address
   him?
How if perchance he knows me?—Fathers' eyes
Are keen at spying prodigals afar,
Through fluttering tatters, and begriming dust.—
   Prodigal! What a name! Have I been such?
True **I** was young, and rosy-cheeked, and rich
The night I left: but oh! 'twas not **to** plunge

Into the golden bath of luxury,
Or play the spendthrift. Bitter tears rolled down,
As sobs heaved panting from my breaking heart.
His word, who, on the Galilean sea,
Reft John from Zebedee, and changed his love,
Alone could have sustained me in that hour.
'Twas He who said; " Leave *them* and follow
   Me ! "
   But see—the door is opening—who comes forth?
'Tis he ! my father ! Heaven give me strength !
[*Stands aside.*]

   Enter Euphemianus, *who* **sees** Alexius.

Euph. Come! a good omen, on this mournful day,
The saddest anniversary of my house.
Alms and a poor man's prayer will bless its grief.
Yet, though he looks both travel-sore and needy,
He asks no alms: I must accost him then.
[*To Alexius.*]
  Good youth, you seem to be in want and pain ;
Can I relieve you ?
Alex.   Gladly I receive
What maketh rich and poor each other's debtors.
Euph. [*takes out his purse, but stops.*] Nay stay,
   it is not gold you so much want,
  As food and rest. No place of entertainment

Is to be found near **this.** Within my house
You shall partake of both.—Ho! there within!
Alex. [*staying him.*] Pray, good Sir, no!
Euph.   Friend,
  would you rob me thus
Of my first draught of charity's sweet air,
Which breathed at morn, adds fragrance to our
   prayer?
Alex. That balmy oblation you have offered up;
For your first words spoke charity. A crust
Softened in yonder fountain, and for bed
This marble seat, will give me food and rest.
Euph. Nay, **friend,** it shall not be. **I** have not learnt
My gospel so, that **a poor man** shall lie
At my gate, wanting crumbs, sore, clad in rags,
While I, in purple raiment, feast within.
Alex. But Sir, I am a palmer, used to sleep
On the bare ground,—
Euph.   **So** much the more I wish
To have **you in my** house for a few hours.
Since **you, no doubt,** have visited abroad
Shrines, sanctuaries, and venerable places:
And have stored up some holy histories,
Which I should love to hear.—
Alex.   Some such I know,
And later **will wait on** you, **to** relate.

Euph. No, friend, it shall be now. While I but go,
  For holy rites, to Blest Sabina's church
  Next to my house, do you go in, and rest.
Alex. [*aside.*] Thank heaven! he hath not discovered me.
Euph. [*goes to the house door.*] Come forth here
  some one!

    Enter Proculus.

Proc.   I am at your bidding.
  [**Looks** *suspiciously and contemptuously at Alexius.*]
Euph. Good Proculus, take in this holy pilgrim
  And give him of the best.
Proc. [*coldly.*]   It shall be done.
            [*To Alexius.*]
  Comest thou from afar?
Alex.   Last night I landed
  At Ostia's quay, from Syria's sacred coast,
  And, in **the** cool of night, gained Rome and
    Aventine.
Euph. Then truly you need rest: Proculus, hasten,
  And let a chamber quickly be prepared.
Proc. It is impossible! And for a stranger—
  One utterly unknown! [*To Alexius.*] Was there
    not plague in Syria,
  When thou didst there embark?

Alex.   None that I heard of.
But I'm aware I am myself a plague,
In such vile rags, unfit for dainty chambers.
Let me repose beneath these shady trees.

Proc. [*drawing Euph. aside, while Alexius retires.*]
Sir, as an old, I trust a faithful, servant,
Let **me** speak freely. **It is rash** and dangerous
Thus to give lodging, even for one hour,
To such a thing as that. There may be a plot
To rob or murder;—there may harbour in him
Deep-lurking maladies,—nay foul contagion
From Asia's swamps, or Afric's tainted coast.

Euph. And yet **the day** will come, when One shall say,
" I was a stranger, and you took me in,"—
Yes; One who lurks in the outcast and the beggar
Will speak thus to the rich.

Proc.   Then not to you.
Doomsday will find **you** poor. Your lavish alms
Would **eat** up your estates, were they twice
    doubled.
Forgive plain speaking. Through the day and night
This is my anxious thought!

Euph.   Nay call it godless!
For blessed charity is not a canker,
Which gnaws, like vice, into our paltry wealth:
Charity is not rust, nor moth, nor robber.

But holy alms are like the **dew of heaven,**
A moisture stolen from the field by day,
Repaid with silent usury at night.

Proc. [*peevishly.*] Then be **it so.** I will procure
him food.

Euph. And place **of rest.**

Proc. Where, Sir?

Euph. No matter **where,**
So that it be where charity suggests.

Proc. We have no chamber vacant, but—

Euph. **Go on.**

Proc. The one **which this** day five years was left
empty.

Euph. Rather mine own than that. None shall lie in it,
Till poor Alexius rest him there again.

Alex. [*starting.*] Once more I pray you—

Euph. Not another **word,**
But follow Proculus within. **I** fear
I've been, through too much courtesy, uncourteous.
What is your name, good friend?

Alex. *Ignotus,* Sir.
I pray you, let me bear you company
To the fair temple of Sabina. There
Would **I** fain sanctify this day, to me
Most blessed at its dawn, now doubly blest
In my thus meeting you.

Euph.   I bid you welcome.

                             [*Exeunt together.*

Proc. Smooth, canting hypocrite!—but I will foil
     thee!

    Twine round his soft old heart—thence will I
      pluck thee!

    Come with **him to his** house—out I will drive
      thee!

   No, not six hours shall this new friendship last,

   The "Unknown" shall be thy *future* name, if not
     thy past.   [*Exit.*

Scene II.—*The* **Atrium of** *Euphemianus's house. The street door* **at the right of the** *stage: the entrance to the interior of the* **house on** *the left. In the middle,* **at** *the back of the stage,* **a** *small room with closed door, under a staircase. A table in the middle covered with a cloth reaching to the ground; behind* **it an** *arm chair.*

Enter Bibulus *from the house side, cautiously looking round; then he turns towards the door.*

Bib. It's all right, all right, **come** in. The coast is clear, and will be, **for** at least a good hour.

Enter Ursulus, **and** *all the other slaves, white and* **black,** *first timidly, bearing various utensils of* *household, garden, and stable work, ladles,* **brushes, rakes,** *curry-combs, &c. They range themselves* **on** *either side,* Bibulus *going behind the table. After the others,* Eusebius *enters quietly, holding* **a book,** *and stands in the back-ground.*

Urs. What have we been **all** brought together for?

Bib. You shall hear presently.

Dav. Stay **a moment: for there is no** *Nostrum** **pre**pared, for **you** to *dress* **us** from. So I will **make one.** [*Turns the chair round and* Bibulus *mounts it.*] Thus I make one out this *crural†* chair, that is to say, an *arm-chair,* you see.

Bib. Now, comrades, **I am** come to speak **to you** about our manifold wrongs. I have been shamefully treated. Of course, when I say shamefully I mean shamelessly.

Several. How **so?**

Bib. How so? **Why I have been** shut up **all** night **in** a dungeon—in **a cellar—a** dry cellar mind, together with empty barrels, carcasses from which **the** spirits had long departed; and I have **been** bitten all night by mosquitoes. And **all for** nothing!

All. Shame! shame!

* Rostrum. † Curule.

2

Bib. Will you stand this? Will you allow your rights to be thus trampled on?

Dav. Rights? Why you said you came to speechify to us about our wrongs; and now you talk about our rights. Which is it?

Bib. Booby! Do you not know that the more wrongs **a man** has, the more rights he has? **He must have all his** wrongs set **to** rights.

Verna. To **be** sure, Bibulus makes it quite **plain. All** wrongs are all rights. Aren't they?

Bib. Exactly.

Dav. **And** therefore **wiser worser, all** right **is** all **wrong.**

Bib. That's it. **That's your** modern *plitical conomy.*

Verna. So right or wrong, **it's** all **one.** Hurrah!

All. Hurrah! hurrah!

Bib. **So it was** right you see,—no **it** was wrong—let me see, well it was either right or wrong, as the case may be, to keep **me in** prison all night; and so your rights were wronged in me.

Urs. But you **haven't** told us what it was for.

Dav. Aye, **tell us *our*** rights that ***you*** were wronged **for.**

All. Yes, yes! what was it for?

Bib. **Why** for a **paltry** flask **or two of** wine, which I drank to master's health.

Ver. **Then if** I understand the matter, **we** were wronged in not having our share **of it**. That was **our** right; and **it was** *you* who wronged us! Down with him!

All. Aye, down with him! [*They rush towards him.*]

Euseb. [*laughing, steps* **forward to** *check them.*] Come, friends, enough of this folly. The long and short of the matter is, that **he** walked into his master's **hock,** and so the master walked him into his **quod**. That's a perfect concord, agreeing **in gender, number and** case; and therefore **if** one agreed with *him* **the** other did too.

Bib. **I** think it's the wrong case altogether; for certainly *hock* agrees with me, and *quod* doesn't! But let us have common sense, and none of this cram!

Dav. Yes, yes, Bibulus is right—common sense, now! Let us by all means have common sense.

Euseb. Very well. Let me ask, is not the wine the master's **property?**

Several. **Of course it is.**

Euseb. He has **a** right to keep it in an amphora **in his** cellar.

Bib. Aye, **till** we can get at it.

Euseb. Hold your tongue till I have done. And if it be poured, as usual, into a sheep-skin, may he not still lock it up **in** his inner cellar?

Sev. Certainly, what then?

Euseb. **Or if into an ass's skin, does that make** any difference?

Sev. Of course not.

Euseb. Then that is just the case.

All. **How?**

Euseb. **Pray what** is the difference between its getting **into Bibulus's** skin, and into any *other* donkey's skin? Had not the master an equal right to lock it up in his cellar? And that's just what he did.

All. Bravo, bravo! Bibulus is an ass.

Bib. [*furious.*] **I'll** pay you **out** for this, one day, Eusebius. **Listen,** my friends. **All** this comes of bad logic, as **one may say:** of putting the premises before the consequence. I'll teach you right logic. Pray what was wine made for?

Urs. **To be** drunk, of course.

Bib. Well then, let that wiseacre tell you, how wine **is** *to be* **drunk, without** *being* drunk.

Ver. Very **good.**

Bib. Then **you see, in** being drunk, I only did what wine was made for: *ergo,* I did quite right.

Dav. **And** therefore quite wrong.

Bib. **But** the fact **is,** the **wine is as** much mine as Euphemian's. **Who** gave *him* the soil? Who gave *him* the vines? Nature made them both, and nature gives them as much to me as to him. Before nature we are all equal.

All. To be sure we are!

Bib. Then why is not the wine mine as much as Euphemian's?

Euseb. Because you did not make it.

Bib. Neither did he.

All. True, quite true!

Bib. One man has no right to the produce of many others' labour! If we are all equal, it is clear that all things should be in common! Down with artificial distinctions, say I. Why should one man wear broad-cloth, and another long-cloth? One drink Falernian, and another Sabine? Tell me that!

Euseb. Come, Bibulus, you are getting venomous. Let us be equal. Why should you stand on a chair, and we on the ground? You have all the talk and we only listen?

Sev. Go on! go on!

Verna. [*shaking a rake.*] I like this wholesale way of levelling; it beats rake husbandry hollow. But how could we make a right division? Lay all out in flower-beds, as one may say.

Bib. Oh, very easily. You should have the garden: Eusebius might take the library, and welcome.

Euseb. Thank you, and how live?

Bib. Why, **haven't I** heard you say that you *devour* new publications, **relish a** good poem, and would like to *digest* a code of laws? Haven't you often declared, that in a certain book there was want **of** *taste,* **that** another was a *hotch-potch*—that one **writer was** *peppery,* **and** another *spicy,* a third *insipid,* or that, poor wretch! he had been terribly *cut up,* or made *mince-meat* of, and completely *dished* by those cannibals called critics?

Dav. Bravo, Bibulus; you have settled *his* hash, **at** any rate. **Now** for the rest.

Bib. Well, then, Strigil might have the stables and horses, Fumatus the kitchen, and I—the cellar.

Sev. **No, no:** that **must** be common property.

Urs. This is all very fine: but how are we to get **at** our own? Would Euphemian do it kind, and give up?

Bib. [*hesitating* **and** *deliberating.*] Well, on that point, **I do not clearly** see my way. Belling the cat, eh? I can't see, unless we set the house on fire—

Urs. Nay, that would be destroying all our property.

Bib. [*aside.*] Except the cellar. [*Aloud.*] Still that **would be** a noble way of asserting our rights.

Dav. To be sure it would, and it would be great fun!

Euseb. Come, Bibulus, enough of this fooling. You are now becoming mischievous, and treacherous too. My friends and comrades, you cannot be so mad as to dream of such wickedness and absurdity.

Urs. [*doggedly.*] Well, then, at least let us have the satisfaction of setting some one else's house on fire. It will be some compensation for being trampled under foot **at home.**

Sev. Whose shall it **be?**

Bib. I like the idea, as a sort of distraction, you know, from our own grievances. Let me see. Oh! yes! there are plenty of neighbours not far off. Their people seem tolerably comfortable, and their houses are in good order. But there are some in them that would like to see a good flare up; and why have not we a right to give i them?

Euseb. Why so?

Bib. Why so? Why for fifty reasons. First, they don't eat beef as we do. They *ought* to eat beef.

Ver. So they ought. That's a capital reason; what else?

Bib. **Then they are** not like **us.** Not one of them

dare talk openly of **setting** his master's house on fire, as I do. *We* are free.

Euseb. And **easy.**

Dav. Aye, free and easy. That's the age, Sir. **We** don't care for *Harry's toggery* we are all for *demonocracy.* Aren't we?

All. **To** be sure we are.

Bib. **We** don't mind masters or stewards.—Do we?

All. Not we.

Bib. We'll pitch them all out of the window.— Won't we?

All. That we **will.**

Bib. Beginning with Proc—Hallo! There he comes. [**Leaps** *down and dives under the table.*]

Enter Proculus. *All look sheepish.*

Proc. Well, gentlemen, what is the meaning of this strange meeting in the hall? How come you to be all here, instead of minding your work? Come, speak, some of **you.** I heard noise enough just now.

Dav. Why, Sir, do you see, as this **is** the sorrowful hanniversary of the family, we thought it shootable to hold a sort **of** conwiwial meeting, just to poke up its affliction. **So** we have been talking over our wrongs.

Proc. Your *wrongs?*

Ver. That is our *rights,* you know, Sir.

Proc. Better still. This **must** be some of Bibulus's work. I am sure I heard his voice—where is he?

Dav. He has absquatulated, Sir: but I think he can hardly have **got** a mile off yet.

Proc. He shall be caught in due time, and shall get his deserts. [Bibulus **peeps from** *under the table,* **and shakes his fist** at Proculus, **who** *does not see* **him.** *All laugh.*] What are you all laughing at? He will find it no laughing matter I can tell **you.** However, as you *are* here, I may as well give you a piece of news.

All. What is it?

Proc. Why, that your master has **just now** taken **a** fancy to **a** beggar.

All. A beggar?

Proc. **Aye, a** beggar, **a** man calling himself a pilgrim, whom **he wishes** to bring into the house, to sleep here, **and to eat and** drink of the best. So he commands. And consequently **to** be *dutifully* waited **on by you.**

Urs. That's a downright shame!

Dav. We won't stand it! It's quite beneath us.

Ver. We won't sit down under it! We're quite **above it.**

Proc. [*ironically*.] Oh, **but, no** doubt, you will do all in your power to make him comfortable.

Dav. Oh, to be sure!

Proc. When he is asleep, you will take care to make no noise near, to disturb him.

Ver. **Of** course **we** will!

Proc. And if your master sends dainties to him, you will not intercept them, but will see that he is well fed, and gets sleek and fat.

Urs. Won't we!

Proc. He will have an easy life of it,—won't he, now?

All. Trust us for that! **A** beggar, indeed!

Proc. **Well,** you seem pretty unanimous in that, I think.

Dav. Quite magnanimous, as **you say,** Sir. But where will he lodge, that **we** may know how **to** keep quiet?

Proc. [*pointing to the cell.*] There, under the stairs.

All. Ha! ha! ha!

Dav. He will hardly have a glimpse of light.

Ver. Or a mouthful of air.

Urs. Or room to turn round.

Proc. So he will turn **out** all the quicker.

Euseb. [*aside.*] Why, he is as bad as Bibulus!

[*To Proc.*] Sir, does our master intend his new friend to be so treated?

Proc. Hold your tongue, slave. You are always prating when you are not wanted. My men, you are all agreed?

All. All.

Proc. How he is to sleep?

All. Yes, Sir.

Proc. And to eat?

All. Yes, Sir.

Proc. And to be got out?

All. Yes, Sir.

CHORUS OF SLAVES.

1.

There shall be no rest for his aching bones,
 None to his weary head:
For his bed shall be like the torrent's stones,
 His pillow be as lead.

2.

To him shall his food no nourishment yield,
 Refreshment none his cup:
He shall eat the refuse of garth and field,
 The fetid pool shall sup.   [*Exeunt omnes.*

Scene III.—*The same.*

Enter Bibulus *from under the table.*

Bib. Well! I do think that I am all the better for a little sobering under the table. Really, if I had not given way from a boy to this rascally propensity of mine, I might have been the most popular leader in the Empire! See how, but for that stupid Eusebius, who always spoils everything good, I should have induced those fools of comrades to set the house on fire, and I should have obtained my revenge, and escaped in the confusion. Many a fellow has reached the Roman purple from a less promising beginning.

But as this has failed, let me set earnestly about some other plan. Again and again, I have been vilely used, down to last night. Aye, last night! That was the last drop! That can never be blotted out except by one means.—Yes, in the intense solitude of that foul dungeon,—in the Tartarus of that broiling furnace—in the murkiness of that endless night—still more, in the bitterness of an envenomed soul—in the recklessness of despair— yea, through gnashing teeth and parched throat— I, Bibulus, vowed revenge—fatal revenge. My manacles and gyves rung like cymbals, as my limbs quivered while I uttered the burning words; and a hollow moan, or laugh—I know not which—reechoed them through the vault.

And when did an Asiatic heart retract such a vow? When did it forego the sweet, delicious thought—the only luxury of a slave—revenge?

Euphemianus, thou shalt not be long my master. Yet Euphemianus is a good master—a kind and gentle—Is it so? Then why does he allow me to be lashed every day like a hound—chained up like a ban-dog?

But it is Proculus that doth all this to thee, Bibulus.—And who is Proculus, and what is Proculus? Only the other's arm—his hand—his limb. I strike not at these—I aim straight at the brain—the heart—the soul. I do not maim or cripple—I slay, I kill.

Then, if Proculus die, what better am I? There are fifty worse than he, and ready to take his place.—Here, for example, comes one of them—

Enter Eusebius.

Euseb. Well found, Bibulus, here is something for you. [*Gives him a **paper**.*]

Bib. What is this? You know I am no scholar. [*Trying to read it.*]

Euseb. Why, in two words, it is an order from Proculus, who has learnt your late proceedings, telling you that you are degraded from the condition of a house servant to that of a country slave, and commanding you to proceed this very afternoon to Ardea, there to begin your labours.

Bib. [*starting.*] **To** Ardea! In the very heat **of** summer! To the most pestilential spot in the Roman territory, where the most sturdy perish in **a** year, unless **born** there! Thither am *I* to go —degraded, too!—to die perhaps in a month, like a frog on a mud-bank, when the sun has dried up its brackish pool! Has Proculus thought of this?

Euseb. **Most** certainly; for not only does he know it, but he observed expressly, that this was a more lenient punishment, than being scourged to death, as you had deserved. You would soon die out, he said, and we should be well rid of a pestilent fellow.

Bib. Better **be** scourged to death **with** scorpions, than sucked to death by poisonous insects, or **by a** wasting miasma. Does Euphemian know of **it?**

Euseb. Not yet, but no doubt he will confirm the **award.** Farewell, Bibulus; bear with courage what you have heartily deserved. [*Exit.*]

Bib. Farewell, sycophant! farewell, indeed? **No,** not yet.—There shall be moaning over death in this house, before *I* go **to** encounter it. After this cruel doom, who **will** blame **me,** if I seek to escape it?—Yet here again comes the question—who **is** doing this? Proculus. Then ought not **my** vengeance to fall on *him?* Warily, calmly—let **us weigh** this.

If Proculus dies—Eusebius would be worse. **Now,** if Euphemian dies, it is very different. We know that **by** his will he **has** released all his slaves. So let *him* die, and I am free.

But, is this generous? or honourable? Tut, tut; who has ever been generous, or honourable, with me? **And** am I **to begin** the virtues first? Out upon it—no!

Yet the thing must be done cautiously, securely. **It is an** ugly thing, is killing, even in revenge. One **must** throw **a veil over** it—make **it appear like** an accident, **even** to one's self. Ha! happy combination—I know how **at once to** procure the **necessary** means, and then—the **pilgrim** who is **going to sleep** *there* [*pointing to the cell.*]—Capital! What more likely?—He *has* some design, no doubt—and he **will be the** only person near. A train can **be** easily laid to bring it home **to him.** —Bravo, Bibulus, thou art a clever hand at **mischief.**—By one blow thou shalt gain liberty, security, and—revenge! **Eh?**

Revenge on foes **is** sweet: 'tis **sweeter still,**
When yours is all the gain, theirs all the ill.
[*Exit.*

Scene IV.—*The Aventine.*

Enter Gannio, **in** *rags, with a wallet, affecting to* **be lame.**

Gan. Well, that was **a wise** old poet, Ennius, I think, they call him, **who** wrote those verses,

"**Of all** the trades **in Italy,** the beggar's is the best,
Because **if he is tired,** he can sit him down and rest."

So as **I** drive **a** thriving trade **by** begging, I will **use m**y privilege. [*Sits down, wiping his forehead.*] I have walked twenty miles to get here, for this blessed day, the *doleful* day of the house, so called, I presume, from the liberal alms always doled **out** on **it.**

Enter Bibulus, *unobserved.*

I am well repaid, however, for my diligence and speed, for I am first and earliest in the field. It is clear that none of the fraternity have slipped in between me and the first pickings.

Bib. [*coming forward.*] You are **wrong, there, old fellow.**

Gan. Good morning, Bib; what do you mean?

Bib. Why, that a more knowing one than you has **stepped in before you,** and regularly done you: a **young** beggar, which you are not—a handsome beggar, which **you** never were—and **a** virtuous beggar, which you never will be. He was here when the master first left **the** house, wormed himself into his favour in no **time, and** is invited to **eat,** drink, and sleep in the house—actually in the house. **Orders** are that he must have **the best of** everything. **So** you are cut **out,** at any **rate!**

Gan. [*enraged.*] The villain! all my precedence taken from me; **my `very** birth-right. Every praise you have uttered of him is a sting, **a** dagger to me. Where is he?

Bib. There **he** comes, with **the** master. [*Stands aside while* Euphemian *and* Alexius *pass them, conversing, and go into the house.*]

Gan. Aye, there he goes! a sleek, smooth, treacherous rival!

Bib. Rival? Why, don't you see how completely he is at home with the master?

Gan. That I do.

Bib. You are fairly supplanted *there*, at least.

Gan. I see it. How I should like to—[*makes a gesture of stabbing.*]

Bib. Hush! we all dislike him as much as you.

Gan. I am glad to hear that. But, how can it be managed?

Bib. Gannio, you sell—you know what, eh?

Gan. Powders, to kill rats? [Bibulus *nods.*] Oh, yes, I always have them ready.

Bib. Are they sure in their action, and safe?

Gan. Quite.

Bib. How are they administered?

Gan. You put a pinch of the stuff into a goblet—I mean where the rats drink; and any one,—that is, any rat—that tastes, dies, without remedy, in an instant. No tales to tell—that is, there is hardly time to squeak, you understand; I speak of rats, you know.

Bib. Of course. We should be glad to get rid of—

Gan. A rat, mind you. Recollect, I said so, expressly. I have nothing to do with anything else.

[*Draws a box out of his wallet.*] What will you take it in?

Bib. [*after feeling in his pocket, takes out the paper given him by* Eusebius.] Here, this **will** do. **Is** this enough?

Gan. [*putting some powder into the* **paper.**] Enough for 150 of them.

Bib. And I suppose for *one* beggar.

Gan. **I know** nothing about *that.* But I hope **I shall** never hear of *him* again. [*Exit.*

Bib. **You old** dotard! **Do** you think **I** am going to risk **my** throat to get **rid** of *your* enemies? I have a loftier aim. The fate of Rome's noblest patrician is folded in this little paper. But I have no time to lose. [*Exit.*

Scene V.—*The Atrium.* **A table** *rather on one side, so as to leave the door under the stairs free.*

Enter Euphemianus *and* Alexius *conversing.*

Euph. Have you, perchance, Ignotus, ever met,
Or in your travels heard **of, a fair** youth,
By name Alexius?

Alex.   No uncommon one—
Hath he no token whereby to distinguish him?

Euph. None, except that **of a** sad history—

He was the son of an illustrious house,
Daintily bred, **and heir of** boundless wealth:
Yet as an angel gentle, sweet and pure.
By all beloved — by one too highly prized;
So heaven took him from **him.**

Alex.   Did he die, then?

Euph. **Alas!** far worse than that: he fled from home,
Leaving his parents desolate and crushed.
His mother melted soon away in tears,
And murmured, **as** she patient died, his name.
[*Weeps.*]
This day completes his father's five years' woe.
[*Looking hard at* Alexius.] Methinks he must be
now about your age.
Perhaps a little **taller—no,** the same. [Alex. *tries
to turn away.* **Euph.** *holds him* **and** *looks in*
his *face.*]
Your eyes remind me, **too, so much of his,**
So blue and mild, like doves',—but **he** was fair,
As Phrygian marble, veined with purple blood.—
Yet travel may have browned his cheek like yours.
His graceful mouth—yours is, no doubt, such too,
But that your beard conceals it—had a trick
So sweet, **so** winning, that **by it** alone
I could discern **him** from ten thousand.—**Ah!**

You weep, good pilgrim, too: thanks for those tears!
Oh tell me, then, did you e'er hear of him?
Alex. [*confused.*] Ah! yes, dear father!—I had almost said,
You look so kind—Yes, venerable Sir—
I do remember somewhat—let me see—
Euph. Speak! say, for heaven's sake, what you remember.
Alex. [*sadly.*] It is not much, I fear.
Euph.   Still let me hear it.
Alex. I recollect how to Edessa came,
Some four or five years past, well-furnished servants
Of a great Roman lord, in quest of him;
For I, with many, did receive their alms.
Euph. [*sighing.*] And is this all? Alas! they found him not,
And soon returned, to whet his parents' grief.
Yet do I hope against all hope. His place
Is daily kept unfilled at every meal,
His chamber, swept and garnished, nightly waits him,
Whom day or night, a love unchanged will greet.
Alex. True, faithful love is this! Yes, good Euphemian,
Hope still, and hope: your boy will yet return.

Euph. Ah! think you so? Or say it **but** to flatter
A father's longing?

Alex. 'Twould but ill become me
Thus to requite **your** love.

Euph. **My** love? **What love?**

Alex. That hospitable love, which oft before
Hath harboured angels, why not then a son?

Euph. Thank you, Ignotus, may your words prove
true.
I fain would learn from you your parents' names,
Where you were born, where you have spent your
youth.

Alex. [*aside.*] Heaven protect me!

Euph. Well, another time,
For now, 'tis indiscretion on my part
To keep you from your needed rest—Here comes
Who shall conduct **you to** it. Heaven guard **you.**
[*Exit.*

Alex. And be it blest, this trial now **is over,**
All else **seems** light.

Enter Proculus, **who sets** *down refreshment.*

Proc. **Sir** palmer, I fear you must be weary. Your
chamber is prepared, though **it** is not such as I
could have wished.

Alex. **Any** hole or corner is good enough for me.

Proc. Well, I knew you would say **so**, wherefore I **took you** beforehand at your **word**. You see, though the house is large, its inmates are many.

Alex. No doubt, plead no more, I pray.

Proc. One suite of apartments is never allowed to be occupied; then friends often **drop** unexpectedly upon us, with large retinues—great people, rich people, you understand? *respectable* people.

Alex. I **beg you to** spare all excuses. Anywhere will do.

Proc. As I suppose **you** will only want **a few hours' rest**, **and then** will resume your pilgrimage, **a small** chamber, and not very luxurious couch, **will** suffice.

Alex. Any place, good Sir.

Proc. [*showing him the cell.*] Then would it please you to rest here?

Alex. [*smiling.*] Most certainly—it **is** quite a palace for *me*.

Proc. There is **some** refection **for you**: and may your **slumbers** be refreshing. [*Exit.*

Alex. Is this to be the sealing sleep of life,
  Gluing my eyelids in unwaking rest?
  Shall my heart, ere 'tis over, **cease to** beat,
  And shall my soul awake to heaven **this** day?
  It would appear so; for I now have reached

My place of birth, to hold it some few hours.
Here, then, **must** sound my last—I am prepared.
My lot is now in better hands than mine.
" **Live** we, or die we, we are still the Lord's."—
One prayer may serve for slumber **or for** death.

Our life is Thine, Creator of all flesh,
Living or dying, wakeful or asleep.
The Hand which plays among the chords of life,
Pressing them gently, their vibration stills
To silence, till **It** wake them once again.
That Hand I kiss this day; for It hath strained
The strings of love and pain to utmost tension,
And now will soothe them with Its kindly touch,
To murmur **peace, on** Its paternal palm. [*Kneels.*]

Father! who here this thing of clay didst fashion
Into Thine Image's terrestrial **frame,**
Its dust together hold, or free disperse,
Where rest my fathers, or are outcasts flung;
Make it the earthworm's, or the vulture's feast,
So that from its corruption flash my soul,
Into the **furnace of** Thy purest fire:
Or rather, like a pearl, be gently dropped
Into the abyss of Thy great ocean-bosom,
To seek in vain for surface, depth, or margin,
Absorbed, yet unconsumed, entranced, yet free.

[*Exit into his cell, closing the door.*

Scene VI.—*The same.*

Enter Bibulus, bearing a salver, with a goblet and food, which he lays on the table. In his right hand he holds an ewer, or flagon.

Bib. In a few minutes, Euphemianus will come for his daily morning refection, and will find it in its usual place. He will drink it, taste it more savoury, and higher spiced than usual—and will expire! What an easy and comfortable death!

[*Striking his breast.*] Down, ye growling curs of remorse! Hush! hissing worm of conscience! You are too late—the potion is mixed, and the fatal drug cannot be extracted. And then, remember Ardea—this afternoon—with its death of a mad hound foaming at the mouth, or a viper shrivelled up on a scorching bank. No; no more qualms. What I am going to do is a safe remedy of all my ills—the easiest way of gaining all my ends. And that sums up all the morality I have learnt, in these days of canting virtue!

Now let us look to our pilgrim. [*Takes out a paper, and looks into the door.*] Fast asleep; sleeps like a dead man! [*Goes in and returns.*] I never saw any one so soundly asleep. The paper is quite **safe by his** bed-side. [*Pours out into the goblet.*] I can say the drink was here some time; **and** I cannot be further responsible.—But, here comes the master—O heavens! I wish it were well over! I will stand by, and **the** first to give **the** alarm! [*Retires.*]

SCENE VII.—*The same.*

Enter Euphemian *from the street door.*

Euph. I own I like my guest. His words are sweet;
His looks call up some image I have loved.
Then his affection seemeth almost filial,
Tender and melting at a father's woe.
I feel athirst! [*Takes the cup, and is putting it to his lips, when a solemn voice proceeds from the cell, the door of which has been left ajar.*]

Alex.   EUPHEMIAN, BEWARE!

Euph. [*starting and putting down the cup.*] Was that some play of fancy mocking me?
[*Looking about.*] No one is nigh, 'twas plainly imagination.
I have felt tempted e'en to press **my** guest,
As they of Emmaus their's, to rest with me—
Perhaps declare him my adopted son!—
My lips are parched! [*Again raises the cup, and the same voice is heard.*]

Alex.   Beware Euphemian!

Euph. [*puts down the cup.*] Beware of what? Not
    of this harmless draught?
  Oh no; I know that voice!—'Tis dear Alexius,
  Far off in body—ah! perhaps in heaven—
  Who thus reproaches me, for my unfaithfulness,
  In putting of this pilgrim in his place. [*Passionately*]
  It shall not be, dear son! But oh! why speak,
  And not be seen? Yet still, if thou canst hear,
  My child, this cup of grace I quaff to thee!
    [*Waving the cup over his head. As he is just
    going to drink,* Alexius *rushes out, and dashes
    it from his hand.*]

Alex. Hold! It is deadly poison.

Euph. [*loud.*]   Ho! in here!

    Enter Proculus *and slaves.* Alex. *snatches the ewer
    from* Bibulus, *and puts it on the table.* Alex.
    in the middle, Euph. *on his right,* Proc. *and*
    Bib. *on his left: the rest on either side, for-
    ward.*

Proc. What is the matter? What has happened, Sir?

Euph. Foul treachery and murder have been here.
  My cup was poisoned.

Proc.   Who hath told you so?

Alex. I.

Proc. **How do *you* know?**
Dav. Every drop is spilt.
Proc. Bibulus, you prepared it; speak! or sirrah,
Your life must answer.
Bib. Sir, **the cup** was **pure**
As heaven's dew, when here I left **it.** What
May, in my absence, have befallen, **I know not.**
They who have tampered with it best can tell.
Proc. Whom do you mean? Speak plain, man, out
at once.
Bib. Him who discovered it—how knew he of it?
Poison there is, but in his tongue who sought
Your heart to envenom. Put him to his proof.
Proc. Sir, Bibulus is right for once.
Euph. There seems
Some lack of proof indeed.
Alex. Then here receive it.
[*Draws out a paper.*]
This paper in my room I found—nay, saw it
Hastily dropped there, as I feigned deep slumber.
Know you **it,** Proculus?
Proc. O gracious heaven!
It is the order but some hour ago
Despatched by **me** to Bibulus.
Euseb. [*looking at* ***it.***] · By me
Delivered to him.

Euph. What does it contain?

Urs. 'Tis ratsbane, I can see.

Bib. [*aside.*] Fool that I was! [*Aloud.*]
Assassins may be thieves.

Alex. Then come to proof.
This ewer, Bibulus, was in your hand,
When here you entered; was it not?

All. We saw it.

Alex. [*takes the empty cup left by* Proc. *and pours into it.*] No one with *this* has tampered; drink it then,
Before thy master's eye. [*Offers it to him.*]

Proc. Yes, drink it off.

Bib. Before his feet to die! Good master spare me! [*Kneeling.*]

Euph. Oh, heavens! Thanks for such a mercy.

Proc. Sir,
Let punishment condign requite this crime.
Seize him, and bind him fast, for death.

All. Aye, aye, Sir.
[*They rush on him.*]

Alex. [*interposing himself.*] Sir, in exchange for *your* life saved, I ask,
Give him to me, or rather to your son,
On this his mournful day.

Euph. I can't refuse.

Alex. And now for my reward—

Euph. Ask what you please.

Alex. Your purse!

Euph. What! paltry **gold**?

Alex. Yes, yes, indeed,
I never felt **so covetous as now**.

[*Euph. astonished, gives him his purse.*]

[*To* Bibulus.] Take this and flee. **At** Ostia's quay yet lies
A vessel bound to Palestine; there seek
Pardon, 'midst scenes of all forgiving love.

[*Exit* Bibulus.

Euph. **As** yet, Ignotus, all my debt remains
Uncanceled, and must be so. For with life
I owe **to you,** whatever gives **life** worth.
This house, my fortune—all belongs to you.
Be this my first request—we part no more.
We share this roof, through what of life remains.
Where are you lodged?

Proc. An't please **you, Sir,** by reason of some repairs, **and,** and—

Euph. And what, pray?

Alex. I am perfectly satisfied with my quarters, Sir.

Proc. Exactly, **Sir,** the gentleman being anxious for **quiet** and devout retirement,—being a pilgrim, you see, Sir,—

Euph. Come, come, tell me at once—where have
   you harboured him?
Proc. [*confused, and pointing back.*] Why, there, Sir.
Euph. There? In that dog's hole hast thou kenneled
   him?
   Is that the pilgrim's welcome in my house?
   Shame on thee, Proculus!
Alex.   Peace, good Euphemian.
   If I had not lodged *there*, thou wouldst have died!
All. Very true.
Alex.   Now this chamber hath been blest
   To you and me: I claim it therefore from you.
   There will I live, and, if heaven pleases, die.
Euph. Ignotus, I must yield to you. But say,
   How did you learn my danger? Whose voice
      heard I?
Alex. That voice was mine.
Euph. [*aside.*]   It sounded like my child's.
Alex. While in sound sleep, methought there stood
      beside me
   A being fair, but radiant as the morn.
   His purple wings were tremulous with gold,
   Like cedars in the breeze at set of sun.
   He struck my side and woke me. Then I heard
   That slave's foul treachery. He entering in
   With black design, believed me fast asleep,

  And dropped his poisonous bait. I started up,
  And, through **the** door neglectfully unclosed,
  Saw all the rest.

Euph.   A blessing came **with** you
 Into my house.—But say who was that spirit?
 He entered too with you.—

Alex.   I know him well.
 He is the pilgrim's **angel, he** who wards
 The hospitable threshold.—Mark my words.

  Four angels guard our gracious works of love,
 Guide them below, and chronicle above.
 The fainting, feeds from silver bowls the first,
 With golden cup, the second slakes their thirst.
 The third the naked clothes with broidered pall;—
 But HOSPITALITY unites them **all**,—
 To clothe, feed, quicken, when his jewelled key
 Opens, **for harbour,** home or hostelry.

Him these **three** spirits tend,—him glad surround,
 Who brighter works **of** mercy leaves to them;
While he, with seraph-gaze bent on the ground,
 Finds in the dust, and saves some " hidden gem."
        [*Exeunt.*

END OF FIRST ACT.

ACT II.

There is an interval of five years between the first and second acts.

SCENE I.—*The* **Atrium.** **Enter** Euphemian, Carinus, *with* Eusebius, *in cloaks and petasi, or large hats.* Eusebius *takes off their travelling attire, and* **goes** *out.* Car. *has the bulla round his neck.*

(*A couch, raised only at one end, in the apartment.*)

Euph. Well, dear Carinus, are you tired?
Car. No, father;
 (Since I must call you so, by your command,)
 This morning's journey has been charming. What
 Could be more lovely than the Tiber's banks,
 Fringed with those marble villas, cool i'th' shade
 Of lazy pines, and scarcely-nodding cypresses?
 All was so still; except the gilded prows
 That shot along the water, bright yet soft,
 As swarms of summer fire-flies.
Euph. Welcome, then,
 To your own goodly home.
Car. [*looking round him.*] A goodly home
 It is, indeed, and fair! **And yet** not mine.

4

Euph. Right: **for** to-morrow is the day appointed
    For your adoption. **Then,** indeed, more truly
    All that you **see** will yours become; and **more.**
Car. **How can** that be, your heir being still alive?
Euph. Alas! all hope is now extinct!
Car.   **How so?**
Euph. **I** have in vain **the** whole world travelled
      through,
    Made proclamations, offered high rewards,
    And more **than all,** have trusted to the instincts
    Of filial love, wherever it might be,
    To claim its **dues.**
Car.   **If** heaven had stronger claims
    All this was vain.
Euph.   Only three days and nights
    Did Mary's Son allow the quest for Him,
  By His dear parents—full ten years has mine.
Car. O Father! those three days were *twenty* years
    To Mary's heart!
Euph. [*aside.*]   What wisdom hath this child!
  [*Aloud.*] My hopes are wearied **out.** Therefore
      to-morrow,
    The anniversary of our long mourning,
    Shall mark our change to joy. Honorius comes
  To honour my poor banquet. At its close,
    Amidst the clang of trumpets and of cymbals,

  The Emperor himself will name you heir
  Of all your uncle's wealth.
Car.   And if Alexius,
  Before the echo of those sounds be quelled,
  Appear amongst us?
Euph.   No. It cannot be.
  Conjure not up such fancies. For five years
  I have been buoyed up by the hopeful speech
  Of a young holy pilgrim, who yet dwells
  Within these walls. Ten years is long to hope!
Car. But tell me, father, was Alexius all
  That I have heard described? Gentle and sweet,
  Obedient, pure, to the distressed most kind,
  To saints devout, burning with higher love?
Euph. All this, and tenfold more, if ten times told.
Car. Then let me be the sharer of his virtues,
  Never usurper of his heritage.
  Alexius lives, and will claim back his own.
Euph. How say you, child?
Car.   You have described a saint,
  Such as dies not, but all the Church shall know it.
  Remember how, when Servulus, the mendicant,
  Died in the court of holy Clement's church,
  Our earthly psalmody was hushed, to hear
  The angels chaunt his passing-hymn outside.[*]

[*] St. Gregory's Dialogues, B. iv. c. 14.

Euph. Oh! may it be so! Then will he not care
For worldly wealth or honour!

Enter Eusebius.

Euseb. Pardon **Sir**!
The household are without, anxious **to** pay
Homage to you and to their future lord.
Euph. Let them come in!

Enter Davus, Verna, *and other slaves, and range
themselves on either side.*

Euseb. Your servants, Sir, desire
To welcome you again, after long absence,
And pray you many years of home and joy.
Dispel the cloud which hath so long o'erveiled
The sun-light of the house. Try to forget
By learning how to hope! May this young bloom
   [*Pointing to* Car.]
Upon the household tree gracefully mantle
The winter's past decay.
Car. No, good Eusebius,
Say autumn's ripened fruit. **I'm but** a boy,
And cannot take **the** place of manly virtue.
My friends, I thank you for your kindly wishes,
And as you love me, grant me but this favour;—
I wish not to be courted, flattered, fed

With honeyed speeches. Let me hear the truth
From all, at all times, though that **truth** be blame.
All. Bravo! Bravo!
Euph. Thanks, my good friends; such proofs **of**
    kindly feeling
Bind up a household in strong mutual love.
Haste now once more, **each to** prepare his part
For the glad morrow; when our Emperor
Will grace our board, and our new heir proclaim.
To-morrow's sun shall bleach our **mourning palls,**
And kindle joy in these ancestral halls.
                      [*Exeunt omnes.*

Scene II.—*The same.*

Enter Alexius *solus, faint, and weak—sits down.*

Alex. How long? O heavens! how long shall I drag **on**
  This lingering life? Five years **are on the** eve
Of their completion, since I entered here.
Smoothly **hath** time flowed on, yet quickening ever
Its rapid **course; and** now methinks I am
Like one **who nears a** cataract. His skiff
Glides through a noiseless, foamless, liquid **furrow,**
Which **curves** at last over **the** craggy ledge.
So sweetly calm I feel, **so** lulled to **rest,**
Though **still upon the surging wave.** My heart
Pants audibly indeed, yet does **not** fret.

  Gladly before I die, my future heir
 I fain would see. But once, while yet an infant,
 I stole a glance at him. How years rush by!
 Childhood's best prophecies were written fair
 On brow and lip, illumined by the eye:
 If that first page lied not, the book is rare.

  Enter Eusebius, *bearing a dish.*

Euseb. Good day, Ignotus, I have longed to see you,
 Since our return. My noble lord, Euphemian,
 Now gives me cause. Accept from him this food,
 Prepared for his own table. But, good heavens!
 How sadly altered you appear! Art ill?
Alex. I am but passing well.
Euseb.   I fear, Ignotus,
 That in our absence you have suffered much
 From the unruly, ill-bred slaves.
Alex.   Oh! no.
 For it would ill become me to complain,
 Who was sent here to practice deeper patience
 Than ever hermit in his desert grot.
 Its end is near!
Euseb.   What mean you, friend Ignotus?
Alex. You soon will know. But tell me of this boy.
Euseb. Carinus?

Alex.   **Yes.** Is he a worthy heir
To good Euphemian?

Euseb.   I would almost say
To best Alexius. But yourself shall know him.
For much he longs to hold some converse with you,
Bred up himself in Asia.

Alex.   Haste to bring him.

Euseb. [*going.*] I go to seek.

Alex. [*taking up the dish.*]   While I these dainties bear
To Gannio at the door; he loves them dearly.

    As he is speaking, enter Ursulus, *meeting him.* Euseb. *stops suddenly at the door* on *the other side, and looks from a distance unseen.*

Urs. Hallo sirrah! whither so fast with that nice dish?
Give it up instantly!

Alex. Willingly, pray accept it from me!

Urs. Accept indeed, what belongs to me! What right have you, a beggarly intruder, to intercept what, of right, belongs to the household? I will not accept, I take it. [*Snatches away the dish, and pushes* Alex. *rudely,* who *staggers backwards on the couch, and rises again faint, standing in the middle.* **Just at** *this moment* Carinus *enters,* *opposite to* Eusebius, *and starts at seeing this act, but retires to the back of the stage, and remains unseen behind a pillar.*

Euseb. [*rushing forward and seizing the dish.*]
Avaunt, foul harpy! ravenous, impure! Defiling what thou touchest!

[*He pushes him across the stage, so that he staggers against Proculus entering. Then puts down the plate.*]

Proc. How now? slave.

Urs. Eusebius, **Sir,** pushed me against you, after snatching a dish from me, which I was bearing from Ignotus to Gannio.

Euseb. He lies, Sir, foully.

Proc. **Peace, thou** forward slave!

Euseb. No more than thou a slave.

Proc. Ha! dar'st thou, sirrah!

Euseb. Sirrah me, sir, no more! I'm free as thou.

Proc. We'll see just **now.** Come Ursulus, say on.

Urs. I say then that it's all along of that interloper Ignotus. Since he came into the house there has been no peace. We have had nothing but quarrels on his account. And Eusebius has always taken his part, in spite of what you bid us, five **blessed** years ago.

Proc. Thou sayest true. Like a needle or an arrow-point imbedded in the flesh, is a stranger that

thrusts himself into **a house. Wherever it moveth**
it causeth irritation and pain.

Euseb. And pray did *he* intrude himself, or did the
master of the house invite, nay press him?

Proc. What care I? so he's here against *my* will?

Alex. Nay, but I knew not that it was so, Proculus.

Proc. You must have been most stupid, then.

Alex. How so?

Proc. Could you not see, before you had been here
A single hour, how I had vowed a vow,
That not five more you should remain?

Euseb. That vow
Proved false as he who made it.

Proc. Silence slave!

Alex. Had you but told it, never would Ignotus
Have stood between it and fulfilment.

Proc. Then
Here I renew it: shall it be fulfilled?

Alex. Surely; to-morrow I go hence.

Euseb. No; never!

Proc. I take you at your word, Ignotus. Go!

Urs. Aye to the gallows, if you like, false palmer!

Proc. To-morrow, by this hour—

Urs. Make yourself scarce.

Alex. It shall be so.

Euseb. I say it shan't.

Proc.   Why not?

Euseb. 'Twill be a day of joy.

Proc.   Doubly, without him.

Euseb. 'Twill bring a curse upon the house—

Urs.   A blessing!

Alex. Peace friends! Like Jonas, cast me into the depths
  Of seething ocean, to restore your calm!
  But let me reckon with you ere I go.
  Ursulus, tell me, wherein have I wronged you?

Urs. Why, in merely being here. You are an eyesore to me, a blotch, an excrescence, an ugly wart. **Do these** things wrong any one? Yet, who can bear them? Whom does a spider hurt, or a house-lizard, or a centipede? Yet who does not loathe and hate them? [*Savagely.*] Who would not gladly **set** his foot on one of them when he sees it, and crush it thus. [*Stamping.*] Their offence is merely their presence, their existence! And that is yours.

Alex. [*smiling.*] Well, my existence is beyond my reach,
  My presence I have promised to relieve you of.
  Now, Proculus, with you a parting word.
  Be it in peace!

Proc.   Aye, peace eternal!

Alex. [*mildly.*] Proculus,
You have not squandered gentleness on me,
Nor lavished kindness, since I entered here.
I speak not to reproach; you did not mean it:
Nor am I worthy of aught better.

Euseb. Oh!
Speak not thus, good Ignotus. You have been
Foully misused.

Proc. Peace, slave, I say again!

Alex. Forbear Eusebius; well, I know myself,
[*Carinus draws nearer, still unnoticed.*]
Friend, [*To Proc.*] have I ever murmured a complaint,
E'en to the winds, much less to others' ears?
Have I not bent me enough to your reproaches,
Bowed lowly enough before your scorn, or sunk
Not prostrate quite, beneath the sullen blow,
Or stinging buffet of you, or your servants?

Proc. Hold, villain, hold,—

Euseb. The "villain" in thy **teeth**!

Alex. Eusebius, if you love me, silence! Proculus,
Say if in this I have not so demeaned me
As hath well pleased you, and I'll crave your pardon.
If I have not been meek enough and humble,
If I have scandalized some weaker brother,

By haughty bearing, while within this house,
Tell me, that to the very dust, I may
Stoop before you and him, and part forgiven.
Euseb. Nay, 'tis for *him* to ask your pardon.
Proc.   Bah!
You came to act a part, and **well have** acted!
The sleek and smooth-faced palmer, unrepining
At a snug berth. Some patience is good pay
For five years' shelter, clothing, food, and alms.
Where is the beggar that can't bear a taunt,
Aye, or a blow, for one coin? But five years'
Living, upon the sweat of others' brows,
Must be a beggar's paradise!
Euseb.   Shame! shame!
Proc. Aye, shame enough! **that a** young sturdy vagrant
Should eat the bread of honest, toiling folk.
Urs. Honester than himself, I'll warrant you.
Proc. Shame, that he should be sitting all the day,
As if at home, within another's house,
Instead of putting out his strength to interest,
And drawing food from his strong sinewy arm.
Urs. Pampered, too, with the best of everything!
Proc. **Can I,** who **bear** the burthen of this house,
With patience see **a** lazy parasite
Feed on its fatness? suck its very blood?—

Now, hear my answer: under just reproach,
Scorn well deserved, blows richly merited,
You may have wisely bent—not **low enough**
By one good fathom, for my deep disdain.
Alex. Can I go lower than the dust?
Proc.   Beneath it!
Alex. Your wish may be fulfilled.
Proc.   No, no; to-morrow
You go to seek elsewhere your grave. Meantime
Thus do I flout you. [*Snaps his fingers in* **his**
    face.]
Urs. [*shaking his fist before* Alex.] And I thus.

              Enter Euphemianus.

Euph.   How now?
Insult you **thus my** guest?
Euseb.   **O were** this all, Sir!
Proc. Silence, thou slave!
Euph.   Slave! He is now my freedman,
And **so your equal.**
Proc. [*confused.*]   Sir, I knew it not.
Euph. What **then?**
Proc.   **I saw him striking** Ursulus,
Himself methought a slave.
Euseb.   Sir, it is false.
This Ursulus was rudely plundering

Ignotus of the food you sent to him,
And I but rescued it.

Urs. O foul untruth!
I heard Ignotus say he wished it taken
To Gannio; so I took it.

Euph. **What has this**
To do with what I saw?

Proc. 'Tis that these two
Make common cause to worry all your household,
Leave it no peace, no rest. And I must own,
I let my feelings carry me too far,
When you surprised me.

Euph. And you, then, Ursulus?

Urs. My tender feelings **too** were wounded, Sir,
He called me harpy!

Euph. **Who?**

Urs. Eusebius.

Euph. Then why revenge yourself upon Ignotus?

Euseb. Give me your ear a moment, Sir.

Proc. Nay, first
Listen **to** me, I claim my right.

Euph. Proceed.

Proc. Ignotus, Sir, did sore provoke me first.
He taunted me with having scorned, ill-used him;
After five years of hospitality,
Spoke **of** himself as of an injured man.

Car. [*from behind.*] O lying villain!
Proc. [**startled.**]　　　　　Did I **hear a** voice?
Euph. 'Twas but an echo. Saith he true, Ignotus?
　Speak, friend, and ease my soul. [*Pauses.*] **You**
　　will not say?
Euseb. I will speak for him. It is a false tale
　From first to last, that Proculus hath told.
Proc. 'Tis true, Sir, every word. Speak Ursulus.
Urs. If it's not true, I never spoke the **truth.**
Proc. See then, what I assert, Sir is—
Car.　　　　　　　　　A lie!

　　　All start; *Proc. and* Urs. *tremble.*

Euph. Methought I **heard a** sound? It **must be**
　　fancy.
　How shall I judge between such jarring words,
　Such yeas and nays?
Proc.　　　　　Why thus, Sir, Ursulus
　And I agree on one side. On the other,
　Eusebius stands alone—
Euseb.　　　　　Come speak, Ignotus.
Alex. [*to Euph.*] I am not worth disputing thus
　　about,
　For **so** I add affliction to **your** charity.
　Who am **I** that should contradict or one

 Or the other? Pray be reconciled—once more
Be friends.
Proc. You see he bears no testimony,
We therefore stand two witnesses 'gainst—
Car. [*coming forward.*]   **Two.**
I have heard all.
Proc. [*aside.*] 'Twas then his voice we heard,
All is now lost!
Car. From first to last—aye all.
Eusebius **hath** said true—the others false.
Proc. And shall **a** stripling's word decide the case,
Against **two old and** faithful servants?
Car.   Yes.
Father! or rather master **here** of all!
Be **you** our common judge! I know I'm young,
Not **witty**, nor endowed **with** brilliant parts,
With ready thought **or** speech. One gift alone
From infancy I **have** possessed and higher prized,
And cherish still.—
Proc. [*ironically.*] And pray what is it?
Car.   Truth.
My lips have never lied, nor will, Euphemian.
Brutal in speech and action both have been
 To this your holy guest. [*Taking* Alexius's *hand.*]
   Be thou, Ignotus,
My tutor from henceforth, my guide, my friend;

Teach me but half the virtue I have seen
This hour in thee, reserving to thyself
The bloom so exquisite that made it lovely;—
Be thou to me Alexius. He, if lost,
Be in thee found! So like you are in virtue!
And what are learning, **genius**, wisdom, save
The gems wherein to set that peerless brilliant?

Alex. [*moved.*] O dearest child! would I could hear
    thee oft:
To learn and not to teach.

Car.   But you have promised
This Proculus, to leave to-morrow.

Euph.   Is it so?

Alex. It is, and I must keep my word.

Car. [*to Euph.*]   Nay, then
You must command, where I can but entreat.

Euph. Ignotus, hear a father's supplication;—
                            [Alexius *starts.*]
Father to this poor orphan! Stay and bless
This house so long as heaven gives you life.
Promise me this.

Alex.   Most faithfully I promise.

Proc. [*aside,*] Prevaricator!

Alex. [*to Proc.*]   And be true to you.

Euph. How can that be?

Alex.   To-morrow you shall see.

Till then be all forgotten, all be peace.

Euph. Yes, let to-morrow be our day of joy,
That gives a father to this orphan boy,
Restores an heir to these long cheerless halls,
By whose award each of you stands or falls.

[*Exeunt omnes.*]

SCENE III.—*The Aventine.*

Gannio *seated on the marble bench, eating a mess in a bowl. Enter* Bibulus *muffled up, with a hat slouched over his eyes, and a beard. Speaks in a feigned voice.*

Bib. Good afternoon, Gannio, still at your post, devouring all the good things you can get from Euphemian's house.

Gan. Pray who are you that make so free with my name?

Bib. Why, don't you know, old fellow, who I am?

Gan. Old fellow, indeed? I don't know who you are, but I can tell you *what* you are.

Bib. How so, pray?

Gan. By your not letting me know *who* you are.

Bib. As sharp as ever! Well, *what* am I?

Gan. Why, you are an impostor.

Bib. How is that?

Gan. A man who wont let others know who he is, wants to impose on them; and so do you.

Bib. It may be only to you that I do not want to be known.

Gan. Then I can tell you that you are worse.

Bib. What?

Gan. A villain.

Bib. [*laughing.*] Ha! ha! ha! how do you make that out?

Gan. Any one who knows Gannio, as you evidently do, and is ashamed of being known to *him*, must indeed be a villain of the first water.

Bib. It is still the same quaint old thing. [*Pulls off his disguise.*] Look at me now! Dost know me?

Gan. Aye, do I, and for worse than either impostor or villain.

Bib. Nay, then, for what?

Gan. Why, for a fool!

Bib. Wherein, good friend?

Gan. You are that Bibulus who once conceived a great idea—and did not execute it; formed a grand plan—and failed; determined to commit a magnificent crime—and repented; prepared poison for his master—and fell on his knees before him. Bah! I despise such a man.

Bib. Well done, Gannio! game to the end!

Gan. Go to: I loathe a sneaking penitent. I suppose you have been wandering all over the world, and have come back—

Bib. The same.

Gan. I was going to say,—a hypocrite. Well, it is not so bad!

Bib. Now, Gannio, that I see you are as staunch as ever, I will tell you of a better thing than poisoning Euphemian.

Gan. What is that?

Bib. Robbing him.—Just listen. How can a man of your spirit sit outside of a house, begging for its scraps, when there are heaps of gold inside, to be had for—

Gan. Hanging, eh?

Bib. Nonsense, man. You may be rich without risk. To-morrow Honorius dines there, and I know that on such an occasion the table is all laid out the night before. A like opportunity may never occur again, in our time. Let me see—the last time was, the day when that foolish boy Alexius ran away; just ten years to-morrow. I remember the table well. Such plate! none of your shim-sham silver gilt, but real sterling gold, for centuries in the family. Such candelabra, such urns, and huge dishes, and flagons.

Gan. With such wine in them, eh?

Bib. Not yet. We must keep sober over it, Gannio.

Gan. Of course. [*Puts a bottle slung round him to his mouth.*]

Bib. My turn, if you please. [*Drinks from it.*] But we must have assistance. Do you know of a couple of trustworthy villains, Gannio? two honest scoundrels?

Gan. Aye, do I, two as cunning as foxes, and as bold as lions.

Bib. Perhaps too as ferocious as tigers. [Gan. *nods.*] So much the better. What are their names?

Gan. I don't know; but we'll call one of them *First Robber* and t'other *Second Robber*, as they do in a play.

Bib. Aye, but we are not acting a play, surely?

Gan. No, no, Bibulus, a hanging matter is no play. Now so much for our pals. I will secure them; next comes how to manage the *plant*.

Bib. We must meet here at dusk, and I will get you with myself into a neglected cellar at the back of the house. All will be busy opening the huge iron chests, unpacking and cleaning and laying out the plate. Towards morning they will all go to rest; and we will quietly walk into the triclinium, fill our sacks—none of your wallets, good big sacks,—and walk out by the front **door.** The only difficulty is where to stow away the plunder.

Gan. I'll manage that. **In a** back street hard **by lives a** friend of mine. One sometimes, you know, picks up an odd brooch or ring, that has fallen off a person, and needs a friend to dispose of it.

Bib. Good ; he has always the pot boiling I suppose ? But how does **he pay?**

Gan. Why, to tell the truth, only so so.

Bib. What **does he** give for wrought gold, for instance?

Gan. For gold he gives the price of old silver.

Bib. Unconscionable villain ! How *can* people be so dishonest ! **And for silver?**

Gan. The value of brass.

Bib. Why *it* is downright robbery ! A complete oppression ! Then for brass ?

***Gan.* Oh, he** would not thank you, even, for any amount **of it.**

Bib. I suppose **he** has plenty of his own already.

Gan. Lots. Then all is arranged. I will go and see my friends. At dusk we meet again. [*Kicks aside his wooden bowl.*] There, out of my sight, **vile** platter—henceforward Gannio disdains all but gold. [*Exeunt severally.*

Scene IV.—*The Atrium.*

Enter Alexius *and* Carinus.

Car. Edessa, then, has been your chief abode,
   During your Eastern pilgrimage. You loved it?
Alex. Dearly; it is a city of much beauty,
   Its houses stately, and its churches gorgeous.
   And then besides it is in truth a place
   Of gentle breeding, and of courtly manners.
   Nor is this all. The east does not possess
   A seat of learning more renowned than that.
Car. I well remember that, in Syria, youths
   Who panted after knowledge oft would say,
   "I will to famed Edessa, there to study."*
Alex. Truly, because each nation hath a home
   Within its walls. Syrians, Armenians, Persians,
   There pass their youth in quest of varied lore.
   From many fountains elsewhere issue rills
   Of letters and of science; some will creep
   Winding along the plain, and dallying
   With flowers of enervating fragrance; some
   Bound sparkling and impetuous from the rock,
   And threaten rudely delicacy of faith.

---

* Edessa, the earliest christian University, had national colleges for eastern nations, at this time.

But in Edessa **these all flow alike**
Into one deep yet crystal cistern,
Filled, **by** King Abgar, with the flood of life
Fresh from its source.*   There they are purified,
Filtered, refined ; and issue, each distinct,
Yet **all** impregnate **with** celestial **lymph.**

Car. **How** marvellous must be this graceful blending
Of the two wisdoms, into **one** design.
 But say, Ignotus, could a boy like me,
With nought **else** gifted but *desire* to learn,
There profit **gain** ?

Alex.   You measure profit ill.
The **vaunt** of youth lies not in ready **wit,**
Shrewdness of thought, or sprightliness of speech,—
Torrents in spring that **leave dry summer** beds,
Trees that yield early, but ill-ripening, fruit.
The grace of youth is in **the** open **brow,**
Serene and true ; in blooming cheeks, that blush
Praise to receive, **but** glow with joy, to give ;
In eye that drinks in, flashes not forth, light,
Fixed on the teacher's lips, as hope's **on** heaven ;
In the heart docile, unambitious, steadfast.—
A youth with **these** may bind a smaller sheaf,
 But every **ear** contains a solid **grain,**

---

* According to primitive tradition he received christianity from its living Founder.

Which heaven's sun and dew have swelled and
  ripened—
Bread of the present life, seed of the next.*
Car. It cheers my heart to hear you talk, Ignotus.
  But tell me more: is there among those homes
  Of solid learning, one which you prefer?
Alex. Where all are excellent, 'tis hard to choose.
  Affection **only may** decide.
Car.   E'en **this**
  From **you might guide** selection.
Alex.   Listen **then.**
  I best remember one of large dimensions,

---

* **The** following may be substituted for the **text,** when elsewhere performed.

Car. **It** cheers me, so to hear you talk, Ignotus.
  But in my heart deep lies a secret thought
  To man yet unrevealed. Your words so sweet
  Would charm **it** from its nest—
Alex.   Perhaps unfledged.
Car. **Yet soon** must it **have wings.** Tell me, Ignotus,
  Can it be wrong in one so **weak as I,**
  To fly at lofty heights, sublimest **aims?**
Alex. [*surprised.*] **What! is** ambition creeping in
  already,

Furnished with all **its** purpose could demand,
A noble **library,** a stately hall,
Art-bedecked cloisters, many-chapeled church.
I often lingered by its walls to hear
Now sacred chaunts, now shouts of youthful glee.
Car. **How is** it called, Ignotus?
Alex.   Near its gates
A lordly yew once spread its boughs; as yet,
Unplumed by time, its hollow trunk there stands,
And gives it name.†
Car.   Proceed, good friend.

To torture your young heart? **So** needless, too!
For yours are wealth, **nobility,** command
O'er a vast apanage.
Car.   Nay, judge me not
So meanly Ignotus; higher far I soar.
Alex. Higher than Rome's first Senator? [*With
    emotion.*] **What**? child,
O no! **it** cannot be!—You cannot dream
To match your flight against the Roman Eagle's,
Snatch the world's sceptre, **and** usurp a purple
Then surely doubly dyed. O **no,** Carinus,
    [*Affectionately.*]

† *Ushaw,* supposed to have thus received its name.

Alex.   It chanced,
  As I Edessa left, that I did pass
    Before its porch, and saw unusual stir,
    Great preparations for a festive day.
    They bid me gently, and I entered in.—
    It was my palmer's privilege. They said
    That day they kept their JUBILEE.
Car.   What meant they?
Alex. 'Twas the completion of just fifty years,
  Since they had there abode.
Car.   A happy day,
  And joyful, must that jubilee have been!

    Such hideous fancies darken not your soul.
    But should their distant pest-cloud but approach,
    Fly from its baleful shadow **as** from death!
Car. O, dear Ignotus, this would be **to** fall,
  With broken pinion, lower; not **to** rise.
  Earth's gifts while scorning, can I love **its** crimes?
Alex. Then solve me your enigma, dearest child.
Car. A nobler name than "Cæsar" or "Augustus"
  I covet: such commands I long to issue
  As angels execute, and demons dread:
  To wear no purple, but what *once* He wore—
  The King that ruled **o'er** Pilate's mocking court:

Alex. Aye, had you **seen those youths'** bright **faces,** heard
　Their ringing cheers, their gladsome minstrelsy,
　Tasted their bounteous banquet, witnessed
　The sacred drama they so well performed,
　In honour of the day, you, though a stranger,
　Would have pronounced it, joyful, happy day !
Car. Indeed I would ! and were there strangers there ?
Alex. Yes, many whom kind courtesy had brought.
　But there were others whom affection drew,
　Or duty **even ;** for they called that house

　To stand before **an** altar, **not a** throne,
　Bearing not the world's lordship, but its Lord !
Alex. [*tenderly.*] O loved Carinus, how my fears have wronged you !
　May heaven's bright blessing beam on your resolve;
　May choicest grace bedew its tender roots,
　Till it grow up to ripeness. But, my child,
　Have you **weighed well** its sequences, conditions,
　Its difficulties, sacrifices, loss ?
　Euphemian **binds to** you, as **its** first link,
　The chain of long succession to his name ;—
　While you would **close it.**

Their mother.   Some were venerable prelates,
And many, holy priests, who once had walked
Along those cloisters, book in hand, to con
Their youthful lessons ; there were many, too,
Who thence had gone to battle with the world ;
And now returned, to thank the very walls
Whence they had plucked their arms.   Gladness
        prevailed,
And mutual gratulation.   All felt bound
In one community of grateful love.
Car. But surely few could measure back that term
Of half a century ?

Car.   But how gloriously !
The priest, like the apostle, *ends* his line,
However proud its nobleness, more nobly ;
As the sun's furnace yields at eve its gold.
Alex. How tell Euphemian this ?
Car.   There is my trial,
And yet to-morrow, it must needs be told.
Will you not help me ? [*Caressingly.*]
Alex. [*looking upwards, and thoughtfully.*]   Yes,
        dear boy, I will.
So noble is your thought, so sweetly told :
So dovelike is your nestling, yet beyond

Alex.   Alas! but few.
 And in the house one only. In the midst
 Of all he sate, uniting old and young,
 Friends of his youth, disciples of his age;
 So that he smiled on all, and made all smile.
 His life the chain, which, threading one by **one**
 The circlets of past fifty years, joined them
 Into one generation. Many hung
 From ring or link;—alone he held both ends.
  So many had he led on wisdom's path,
  So many had sustained up virtue's steep,

 The eaglet I had deemed **it, that if e'en**
 It needed for its growth my **heart's** best blood,
 There, like the pelican, I'd feed it willingly,
 Till thence you drew it forth.
Car.   O speak not so;
 To-morrow **you** shall help me to disclose
 My so long burrowing purpose. [*Hesitating.*] And
  perhaps
 You then will **tell** me your own history.
 Ignotus—pardon—you are not what men
  Take you for. **'Neath** that coarse dress, and in
   that

That by consent they called him all—" the Doctor,"
Aye, " the old Doctor" was their name **of** love.*
Car. O dear Ignotus, you have made me envious
Of other's happiness—but you seem weary.
Alex. I should have been much more, except for you.
Car. How so?
Alex. Because nought is so sweet to me
As to converse with fresh ingenuous youth,
And guide its opening impulses. I fear,
My child, **that** you are wanted; till to-morrow
Farewell!

Spare form, those features wan, there lurks a spark
Of noble nature, and of brilliant fire.
Oh! tell me who you are!
Alex. Yes, **yes**, to-morrow!
Car. To-morrow! Everything on that dark day!
It looks to me like a storm-laden cloud,
Embosoming blight, fever, dark dismay.
And yet athwart **it darts** one precious beam
Of glory, shooting from the deepest hue.
It bears your name, Ignotus, and it shines
Upon my future way.

* The Rt. Rev. **Mgr.** Newsham, President of St. Cuthbert's College.

Car.   That terrible to-morrow ! **But,**
Ignotus, talk to me again and soon,
To-night my dreams shall bear me to Edessa.
Alex. May they be omens of a true event !
You, who **are** young, oh, may you **live to see,**
A second, not a brighter, Jubilee !   [*Exeunt.*

Alex. [*deeply affected.*] Blest be its omen !
But you are wanted—so farewell, my child,
Farewell—who **knows? Yes,** yes, we meet again !
Car. Farewell **until that terrible** to-morrow !
Alex. [*thoughtfully and tenderly.*] 'Twill **not be terrible** when next we meet.
When **our** eyes glass themselves in one another's
Tears will have been wiped from them ; mourning none,
Nor **pain, nor** sigh will be—first things are passed.
Car. Farewell, I'll try to dream, then, of that *bright* to-morrow !   [*Exeunt.*

Scene V.—*The same.*

Night. The stage darkened.

Enter from the house-side, Bibulus, Gannio, *and two robbers. Each is muffled up, and carries a sack heavily loaded, the two robbers have knives or daggers in their girdles. They grope one after another,* Bibulus *leading.*

Bib. This way masters, this way, we are now just at the door.

1st Rob. Which way?

Bib. Why this way.

2nd Rob. But which is this way?

Bib. Follow me, you—

1st Rob. Come, no sauce—where are you?

Bib. Follow your nose, then, straight across the court.

[*At length they meet in the middle.*]

Here we are at last altogether. Now take hold of one another, and follow me.

[*As they do so, a glimmer of light appears from* Alexius's *cell. They turn round, and see him kneeling with his arms extended. They stand in attitudes of amazement, two*

> on each **side; and as** the scene proceeds, one by one **lay down their** sacks, stupified and over-awed. **The** light goes on increasing, till **it** reaches, before the chorus, its utmost bright-**ness.**]

Alex. Ye blessed spirits watch over this house,
Defend its goods and inmates from the prowler;—
And if mine own long-wished-for hour draw **nigh,**
Oh, let me hear once more your minstrelsy.

CHORUS OF UNSEEN SPIRITS.

Angels watch, aloft to bear,
Pilgrim youth! thy parting prayer.
  Into night's dark veil is weaving
    Golden threads **the** coming sun;
  Earth's cold gloom **behind** thee leaving,
    Haste thy course of light to run.
On our bosoms sunk to rest,
Wake **among thy** kindred Blest!

Alex. [*starting up.*] I come, I come, I come;—oh! tarry for me.

> [*The* **robbers** *run away,* **out** *of the house—Day breaking.*]

Alex. [*recovering from his trance, roused by the noise.*]
What means all this, what have we here? Ha! thieves!

'Tis well I watched; what treasures they have
   seized!
The door must be made fast; [*Shuts and bolts it.*]
   and until day
Has roused the slumbering family, this spoil
Will be securer here! [*Puts the sacks into his cell
   and shuts it.*]
                     Well, thanks to heaven!
My poor last will and testament is written. [*Looks
   at a scroll, and puts it back into his bosom.*]
So I am ready. [*A great noise of trampling and
   calling out from the house.*]
                     Ah! the theft's discovered.

Enter Proculus, *and all the* servants, *in great con-
   fusion and with much noise.*

Urs. They must have got out this way. The back
   door is closed, and I have been at it these two
   hours.
Proc. Ah! Ignotus. You too are up betimes; have
   you seen any robbers pass this way?
Alex. No, but I heard them running off.
Dav. [*picking up a spoon.*] Here is proof that they
   have passed through this!
Proc. [*who has been to the door.*] Aye, and more-
   over the front door is bolted and barred; so, cour-

age boys! the robber is still in the house. He shan't escape.

Ver. [*looking into the cell.*] Eureka! eureka! Here's the plunder lads, here's the magpie's nest! **Look,** look!

[*They draw out* the sacks, **and surround** Alexius, *in menacing attitudes,* **and with** *angry gestures.*]

Dav. So you didn't *see* the robbers, eh? **Good reason why,** you had never no looking-glass in **your** room.

Ver. Perhaps if you had had your slippers on, you wouldn't have **heard them either.**

Proc. Well, I think this time, **my good** pilgrim, you will not wind yourself so easily **out of** it : [*Aside*] and that forward boy **is not here to help you.**

Enter Euphemian *and* Eusebius.

Euph. How **now, my men?** It is strange that **the very day, on which my** house **is to be** most highly honoured, **and** I wished it to be **the** most orderly and peaceful, should commence with absolute tumult, as if the place were possessed by evil spirits.

Proc. One at least, **Sir, we have** found ; but **I** hope we shall be able **to** lay **him** effectually this time.
[*Pointing to* **Alexius,** *who is faint and in pain.*]

Euph. What again, and **so soon** after my proclaiming **a truce to your** quarrels till after the festivities **of to-day, are** you insulting **and** assailing the good man?

Proc. The good man indeed! the thief, the robber of your house. [*Showing the sacks.*]

Euph. Good heavens! What means this?

Proc. It means neither more nor less than **that** during **the** night, the most valuable portion **of your** plate, laid **out** for the imperial banquet, has **been carried off,** that the doors are all fastened **inside,** and that we have found it **all in** Ignotus's room.

Euseb. Do not believe so clumsy **a** tale, Sir. Depend upon it, this is only a conspiracy got up against him.

Urs. We are all witnesses to the truth.

All. Yes, Sir, **all** of us.

Euph. **Surely, Ignotus,** this cannot be true? And yet **the** evidence seems strong against you. **This time** you *must* explain. [*Pauses.*] What not a syllable?

Euseb. O dear Ignotus, one word will suffice. Your *no* will answer all their accusations.

Alex. And yet I may not speak it. [*Aside to* Euseb.]

           Good Eusebius,
 My lips are sealed.
Euseb.   **Oh** not by guilt, just heaven?
Alex. **No : by** example, too sublime to name.
Euph. Ignotus, I implore you, speak.—Still silent?
 Speak, **or** I must believe your guilt.—No answer?
 This silence doth condemn you,—wretched **man**—
   [*Sorrowfully and indignantly.*]
  Have I then ta'en a viper to my bosom,
 Whom worthy **I** had deemed to be a son?
 A faithless robber for a holy man?
 And have five years of seeming piety,
 Of feigned austerity, and sham religion
 Been but a hypocrite's **deep** preparation
 For vilest treachery, and meanest crime?
 Who will believe again in human **virtue,**
 If this be true?
Alex.   Oh spare me! mercy! pity!
Euph. Aye, pity me, who have been cozened so!
 Ignotus, had you wanted gold, and told me,
 You should have had it, in its choicest forms.
 I loved you well, and thought I owed you much!
 Now you have shamed yourself, alas! and me;
 Before my servants and my child, have made
 Virtue **a** bye-word, godliness a scorn.

Alex. [*staggering forward.*] Believe it not; but, oh!
   I am so faint,
I cannot speak.
Euph.   Alas! remorse, I fear,
Chokes up your utterance, and saps your strength.
Better confess your guilt by one short word,
And seek forgiveness!
Alex. [*looking about, distracted.*] Oh! where is that
    boy?
Euph. Never shall you set eye on him again,
To blight his virtue by its basilisk gaze.
Go, go, Ignotus, go in peace—for ever.
Alex. [*endeavouring to approach, and kneel before
    him.*]
Oh! spurn me not; by all that is most dear
Still to your heart; by your poor son long lost,
By him who will this day replace him, I
Conjure you, hear me.
Euph.   No, Ignotus, no! [*Motion-
    ing him back.*]
Fly from my sight, thine hour to go hath knelled.
Alex. Ah! now I know 'tis true; Angels, I come!
From other hands I well could stand a *blow*,
The wave of *that* is death. It fills my cup—
To die a thief reputed in that heart,
Where, upon earth, alone I cared for love!

Farewell! [*He sinks back into* Eusebius's *arms, and is laid* on *the couch, raised so as to face the audience. His right hand hangs by his side,* his *left is close pressed on his bosom.*]

Euph.   Let him lie there to gather strength,
Then give him means to go.

Euseb.   Sir, 'tis too late,
His last is breathed on earth.

Euph.   Oh! say not so!
'Twould be an end too horrible; a robber's
Invoking Angels, unrepented, too!

Enter Carinus.

Car. What hath occurred so early to disturb you?

Euseb. See here, my boy, your friend Ignotus dead!

Car. Impossible! Awake, Ignotus, rise—[*Alarmed.*]
It cannot be, what can have killed him?

Proc.   Conscience!

Car. What does that mean?

Proc.   Remorse!

Dav.   He died a thief.

Ver. Just to escape a hanging.

Car.   I'm bewildered!
No, no, his spirit can't be fled. He'll keep
His promise to me, to remain with me. [*Kneeling and taking his hand in both his.*]

Will you not speak to your new pupil? Press
His hand at least. Yours is **yet warm!** Oh give
One token that you know **him!** Ah me! I fear
    [*Bursting into grief.*]
It is too true; some sudden cause hath driven
His soul to an abode more worthy of it.
If so, before high heaven, I protest
Against it loudly, and declare me guiltless.

Euph. [*roused out of deep sorrow, passionately.*]
  Let go that hand, Carinus, lest its touch
  Pollute you, 'tis a robber's, child!

Car. [*looking up, astonished.*]   A **robber's?**

Euph. **Aye, a** blasphemer's, too!

Car.   Blasphemer's?

Euph. One who by his hypocrisy would nigh
  Make us henceforth forswear all virtue!

Car.   How, Sir?
  What can **this** mean? Do you, then, join your
    slaves
  In hateful condemnation of your friend?

Euph. Oh, yes, **at last** plain evidence of guilt
  Hath flashed upon me.

Car.   Though 'twere like the sun,
  I would deny its ray.

Euph. [*pulling him away*] Come, leave that bier
  To its own load of guilt.

Car. What guilt?
Euph. First, theft
  Basest in kind; and after 'twas committed,
  And rank remorse, or heaven's unseen bolt,
  Had felled the culprit, he, without repentance,
  Commended him to Angels' hands.
Car. Enough!
  No hardened villain could have done as much!
  Still less a gentle, saintly youth like him!
  One hour of converse with him yesterday,
  Made me well know him! I dare to proclaim
  His innocence, and challenge all to proof
  Of any guilt in dear **Ignotus.**
Euph. Rash
  And foolish boy, I needs must call you, now.
  Last night this house was robbed of precious plate,
  And there it lies! [*Pointing to the sacks.*]
Car. But, pray, where was it found?
Proc. Within his cell.
Car. [*thoughtful and abstracted.*] And so was
    Joseph's cup,
  Found in the sack of Benjamin—yet, still,
  He was no thief! others may there have left it.
Euph. This is unreasonable—e'en in a child.
  The door was closed and bolted from inside,
  No one can have escaped.

Cur. [*after a moment's pause.*] Eusebius, **Proculus**,
    Haste to the **door**; **fresh** sand was strewn before it,
    For the imperial visit, yester-eve.
    A morning shower hath crisped its surface; see
    If footsteps have yet pressed it. [*They go and
       return.*]
Euseb. Heaven bless thee, gifted boy! the prints are
    clear,
    Of two men to the right, **two to the left**,
    Fleeing from off the **very** door step.
Proc.   Four,
    No doubt, have passed the threshold.
Cur.   And just four
    Are these thieves' **packages**.
Euseb.   O noble youth!
    What instinct have the pure to find the truth!
[*A loud knocking at the door; it is opened. Enter an officer, dragging in* Bibulus *and* Gannio, *handcuffed.*]
Officer. Hath anything happened amiss in your house,
    my Lord? These two men were seen to run out
    of it, and after a hot pursuit have been captured.
    Two others took another direction, and I fear have
    escaped. [*He throws off their hats.*]
Several. Bibulus, I declare!
Others. Gannio, upon my word!

Bib. [*kneeling.*] Good Sir, once more forgive me!

Euph. Surely **I am** bewitched! What means **all**
  this?

Bib. Last night, we two—

Gan. Indeed, Sir, he induced me,
  To join in robbing you, with **two companions.**

Euph. Speak, **one** or other, but go on.

Bib. [*rising*] We filled—
  Aye, there they are—four sacks with plate. **Thus**
    far,
  We had in safety reached.—

Euph. Well, who then stopped you?

Bib. He who once saved your life, **now** saved your
  house.

Euph. **How** so? What **did he?** Speak! my heart
  will break!

Bib. We heard him pray that Angels would protect it;
  Then shone a glory round him like the sun,
  While unseen spirits in a heavenly strain,
  Welcomed him to them. Scared, we fled away,
  As Roman soldiers before Easter's ray.

Euph. **Oh!** wretched man I am! This day I hoped
  Would bring joy, honour, glory to my house,
  Yet hath it bred more grief and anguish here,
  Than any other anniversary.
  Oh! shame **to** have thus spurned the innocent,

Nay, almost cursed him! seen him die, unmoved,
Loaded his corse with ignominy! Oh! blindness,
Not to have learnt after five years' experience,
What one day taught this child, his depth of
    virtue!
My life indeed must now be spent in weeping
Over such guilt!
        But, Proculus, haste, tell
As best you can, the Emperor my grief,
And beg indulgence till a brighter day!
Proc. Stay; for here comes a royal chamberlain.

Enter Chamberlain.

Chamb. Noble Euphemian, I come from Honorius;
  He follows shortly.
Euph.   We are not prepared
  Thus early. Why this haste?
Chamb.   Have you not heard,
  That through the churches of the entire city,
  A voice has clearly rung; "Haste to the Aven-
    tine,
  A saint hath died there!" Crowds are flocking
    hither
  By every avenue. The Emperor
  And Pontiff Innocent have sent me forward,

  To ascertain the spot; **for** no one knows
 Where any saint hath lived, and may have **died**.
Euph. Oh! viler still am I! **A** virtuous man,
 Methought I had misjudged, yet 'tis a saint
  I have held in my house **five years,** nor known him!
 And at his death I have reviled him! Go,
 Pray my good Lords, the Emperor and **Pope,**
 Not to approach the house of one so sinful
 As I have been, till tears have washed my guilt.
Car. Oh! weep not, father, comfort soon will come.
 These, your good **princes, may be sent to bear it.**
 There was a purpose **in this great concealment,**
 A mystery of virtue **unrevealed,**
 Buried in this deep heart;—

      [*Touches* Alexius's *breast.*]
 Ha! and is this its epitaph? [*Draws a scroll
  from the hand on the bosom. All look amazed.*]
      What's here?
[*Opens the scroll,* **looks** *at it, shrieks as he lets it fall,
 and throws himself in passionate grief across the
 bier.* Eusebius *picks up the scroll, and gives it to
 * Euphemian, *who looks at it, drops it, and buries
 his face in his hands,* moaning.]
Euph. O wo is me! deeper my anguish still!
 Keener my shame, blacker my crime! Alas!

That I should not have known **thee**, not dis-
    covered!
That I should have been dead to every throb
Of a paternal heart, deaf to its cries!
Nay, that I should have overlooked the yearnings
Of thy true filial love, to be reclaimed—
(So many instances I now remember)
Looks to me like a spell cast over me.
But, read, Eusebius, read my final sentence.

Euseb. [*who has taken up the scroll, reads amidst profound silence, and signs of amazement.*]

"I am Alexius, son of the Senator Euphemian. A supreme command sent me away from my father's **house**, to wander as a pilgrim for five years. **My** time was chiefly passed at Edessa. After that period, I was similarly commanded to return, and die in the place where I was born. My father's charity has supported me till this my last day.

"I keep **my promises to all.** Proculus, **I depart** hence for **ever.** Carinus, child of my heart, **I** remain with you to guide you still, though unseen.

"My father! mourn not for me; you have secured for me greater happiness than this world **can give. Be** hospitable ever to the stranger: be charitable to the poor. The heir of your house is found **again, as** he has often promised you. But as you decided, *he* should to-day make the award between your **servants,** regarding the pilgrim Ignotus, he hereby pronounces in favour of universal pardon, forgetfulness, and reconciliation.

"Alexius."

Proc. Let me be foremost, **Sir, to** claim this pardon,
As in offending I have been most forward.
Deeply I grieve my past injustices.

All. So do we all.

Bib. and Gan. And we our base attempt.

Euph. All I forgive—but who will pardon me?
Far in the depths of some Egyptian desert,
Must be my shame and sorrow buried. **There**
Tears of repentance may **blot out my guilt.**

[*Kneeling by the* **couch and seizing** Alexius's hand.]

Ah! now I recognize those placid features
In thee, my son, by which I should have known thee!
Here is thy noble brow, serene in grief,
Here are thy truthful lips, smiling in death,
Oh that thine eyes would open;—yet their lids
Can scarce o'ercloud the azure of their orbs!

[*Rising passionately.*]

How blinded I have been! **Oh! who** will draw me
From the abyss of my despair?

Car. [*clinging to* Euph.]   I will.
  Remember, father, 'tis in ignorance,
  And in obedience to a higher will,
  That you have acted. What to you brings sorrow
  Gives him renown on earth, in heaven glory.
Euph. And what is that?
Car.   Why, to have meekly died
  Under false censure of the kindest judge.
  What Isaac would have been, had Abram's knife
  Cleft his unmurmuring breast,—that is Alexius.
  Nay, more; he could not be the saint he is,
  Had he not passed that " *lamma sabachthani :*"
  'Tis the sublimest martyrdom of soul.
Euph. Child, thou hast comforted me! [*To the*
        Chamberlain.] Go, tell the princes
  Who wield the keys and sceptre of both worlds,
  That here reposes one in each most great.
  Myself and my young heir await them.
            [*Exit Chamb.*]
Car.   Father,
  I pray you speak not so. [*Pointing to* Alex.]
      There is your heir,
  Returned to claim his own, and keep his promise.
  All here is his, and he departs no more.
Euph. How shall this be?
  7

Car.   You have no other heir,
  I will be none.   Heaven has called him saint;
  This is his tomb, his shrine, his temple; here
  Must rise a stately church, with ample cloisters,
  To lodge the pilgrim; your estates endow it;
  You be its faithful steward.
Euph.   And Carinus?
Car. Will be its priest.   Till age and law permit,
  He'll seek Edessa.   In (its yew-named)* college,
  Learning with virtue will make years glide quick.
  His diligence shall run a race with yours,
  So nicely matched, that both of you shall win.
  What time the sacred dome shall have been built,
  Its priest from secret study will emerge.
  (For silent toil is youth's best husbandry.)
  Here he will toil in his sublime vocation,
  Console the sorrowing, rejoice the poor;
  The body's ills relieve, but cure the soul's,
  And wing it for the flight beyond all pain.
  Then when the work and griefs of day are ended,
  He'll sit him down beside his cousin's tomb,
  To meditate upon his hidden worth,
  Inglorious virtues, and unhonoured grace,

---

* *Or* (some fair-famed)

    His humble life, and ignominious end,—
    Yet saintly glory !
Euph.   Oh ! Carinus, stay,
    The myst'ry now I read of this great day ;
    Which to my house, through ways by us least
        thought,
    More glory, than all earth's renown, has brought.
    I read its *lesson* too, so high and true ;—
    By him well taught—so be it learnt by you :
    " None in the Church's golden diadem
    Can shine, that is not long, a hidden gem."

THE END.

In the first performance of this Drama, the "Chorus of unseen Spirits" was adapted to the Music of Mendelssohn's beautiful Trio in the Elijah, "Lift up thine eyes." As this is copyright, it cannot be here printed. A new musical composition, which cannot fail to be admired, has been kindly supplied for the song by Mr. SCHULTHES, director of the Choir and Choral College of the Oratory, Brompton: though of course either may be used. Both choruses may be sung without accompaniment.

CHORUS OF SLAVES.

ACT I. SCENE II.

THE HIDDEN GEM. 113

THE HIDDEN GEM. 115

SONG OF ANGELS.

ACT II. SCENE V.

WILHELM SCHULTHES.

The accompaniment of the piano or harmonium is only to be used, in case the voices have a tendency of lowering, it ought to be played pianissimo throughout.

THE HIDDEN GEM. 117

THE HIDDEN GEM. 119

THE HIDDEN GEM.

Haste thy course of light to run, Pilgrim

Haste thy course of light to run,

Haste thy course of light to run,

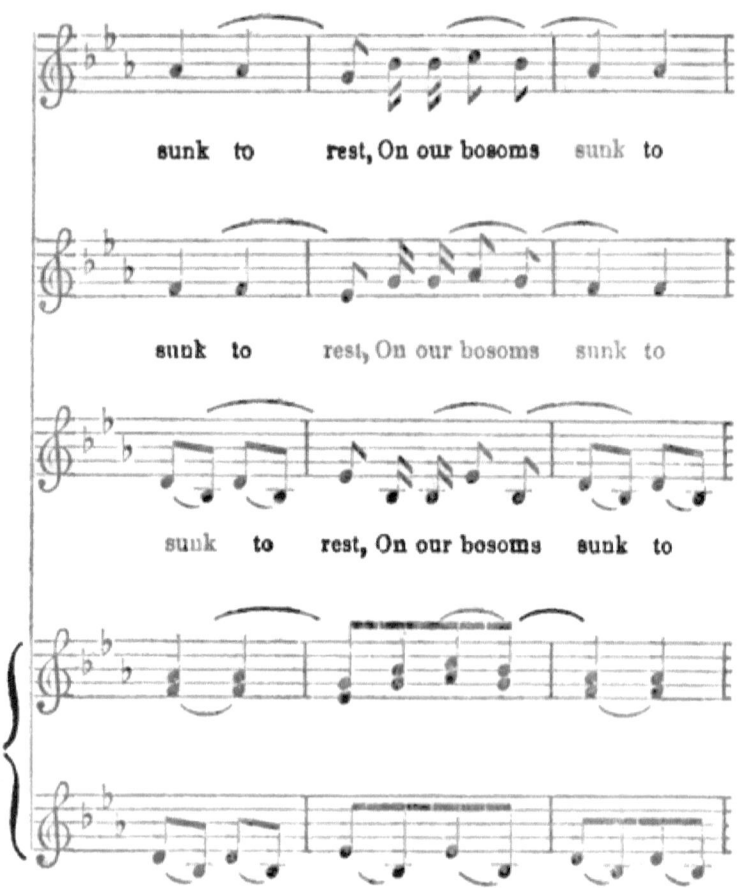

THE HIDDEN GEM. 129

PRINTED BY RICHARDSON AND SON, DERBY.

Published by Richardson and Son.

This day published, uniform with "The Hidden Gem," in printed wrapper, price 4d.

CATHOLIC COLLEGES AND PROTESTANT UNIVERSITIES.

AN ORATORICAL ADDRESS,
SPOKEN AT THE
JUBILEE OF ST. CUTHBERT'S COLLEGE,
USHAW.
JULY 21, 1858.

By the Very **Reverend FREDERICK** OAKELEY, **A.M.**
Formerly Fellow of Balliol College, Oxford.

PUBLISHED BY DESIRE.

This day published, price 4s. 6d.

THE NEW GLORIES OF THE CATHOLIC CHURCH.

TRANSLATED FROM THE ITALIAN
BY THE FATHERS
OF THE LONDON ORATORY,

At the request of the Cardinal Archbishop of Westminster,
WITH A PREFACE BY HIS EMINENCE.

This work, which the Holy Father desires to have translated into all the languages of Europe, contains the ACTS OF THE RECENT MARTYRS OF THE COREA, COCHIN CHINA, AND OCEANICA.

Just Published,

MANUALE VITÆ SPIRITUALIS CONTINENS **LUDOVICI** BLOSII OPERA SPIRITUALIA QUÆDAM **SELECTA**, ad usum præsertim studiosæ juventutis, cura et **studio** CAROLI NEWSHAM, S. T. D., Prelat, Domestic. Sanctitatis suæ, et Collegii S. Cuthberti Præs. Cum Præfatione Emi. et Rmi. CARD. WISEMAN, Archiep. Westmon. Price 5s.

Published by Richardson and Son.

MEDITATIONS ON ALL THE MYSTERIES OF THE FAITH, together with a Treatise on Mental Prayer. By the Ven F. Louis De **Ponte**, S.J. Being the translation from the Original Spanish, by J. Heigham. Revised and corrected. To which are added the Meditations on the Sacred Heart of Jesus. By the Ven. F. C. Borgo, S.J. Translated into English. The last volume contains a copious and valuable analytical Index to the whole. Complete in 6 vols. 8vo., superfine paper, printed wrapper, **18s.**

The First and **Second** volumes are just reprinted, and may be had, price 3s. each, **or** in various bindings at very moderate prices.

Any of the volumes may be had separately, each **vol.** 3s.

CONFERENCES of the Rev. Pere **LACORDAIRE**, Delivered in **the** Cathedral of Notre Dame, in **Paris.** Translated from the French by Henry Langdon. **Dedi**cated to His Eminence Nicholas Cardinal Wiseman, Archbishop of Westminster, with beautiful Portrait, thick demy 8vo., superfine paper, cloth gilt, 15s.

ST. PETER : HIS NAME AND HIS OFFICE as set forth in Holy Scripture. By Thomas W. Allies, M.A., author of "The See of St. Peter, the Rock of the Church," "A Journal in France," &c., demy 8vo., superfine paper, best cloth gilt, **7s.**

DIVINE EDUCATION of the **CHURCH**, and Modern Experiments. By Francis Herbert Nash, A.M. Author of "The Scriptural Idea of Faith," post 8vo. cloth lettered, 4s. 6d.

Second edition, price 2s. superfine cloth lettered, with beautiful frontispiece.

MONTH OF THE SACRED HEART OF JESUS.

TRANSLATED FROM THE FRENCH BY **THE**
REV. GEORGE TICKELL, **S. J.,**

With a Preface by the Translator.

☞ The work from which this Translation is made appeared first in 1836; it is now in its eighteenth edition; and its annual sale amounts to 10,000 copies.

MONTH OF THE SACRED **HEART OF JESUS**, **Selections** from the above Work. **By** the Rev. George Tickell, S. J., Price One Penny.

Published by Richardson and Son.

A NEW WORK BY DR. FABER,
(Addressed to the Confraternity of the
Precious Blood.)

WILL BE PUBLISHED

On Saturday the 18th of February, 1860.

THE PRECIOUS BLOOD;
OR
THE PRICE OF OUR SALVATION.

IN THE PRESS.

Third Edition (**Sixth Thousand**), with an INDEX. **6s**.

GROWTH IN HOLINESS,
Or the PROGRESS of the SPIRITUAL LIFE.

ALSO IN THE PRESS.

Second Edition (**Fourth Thousand**), with a copious Index,
Price **6s**.

SPIRITUAL CONFERENCES.

Ready for the Press.
1. BETHLEHEM.
2. HYMNS AND SACRED POETRY.

Published by Richardson and Son.

NEW WORKS BY DR. FABER.

THE FOOT OF THE CROSS: OR THE SORROWS OF MARY. (With a copious Index.) (Second Edition, 4th Thousand.) Price 6s.

THE CREATOR AND THE CREATURE, OR THE WONDERS OF DIVINE LOVE. Second Edition, (Fourth Thousand,) Price 6s.

ALL FOR JESUS: OR THE EASY WAYS OF DIVINE LOVE. (Sixth Edition, Eleventh Thousand!) Price 5s.

THE BLESSED SACRAMENT; or the WORKS AND WAYS OF GOD. (Companion to " ALL FOR JESUS.") (Second Edition, Fourth Thousand!) Price 7s. 6d.

POEMS. Third Edition. Price 7s. 6d.

SIR LANCELOT. A Tale of the Middle Ages. Second Edition. Price 5s.

ETHEL'S BOOK; or, TALES of the ANGELS. Price 2s. 6d.

An ESSAY on CANONIZATION and BEATIFICATION. Price 3s.

AN ESSAY ON THE INTERESTS AND CHARACTERISTICS OF THE LIVES OF THE SAINTS. Price 2s.

AN ESSAY ON CATHOLIC HOME MISSIONS, printed wrapper, price 1s. 6d.

A LETTER TO THE MEMBERS OF THE CONFRATERNITY OF THE MOST PRECIOUS BLOOD. One Halfpenny.

THE ROSARY; OR THE LIFE OF OUR LORD JESUS CHRIST. Price One Penny.

HYMNS FOR THE PEOPLE, adapted to popular tunes. Price 1d.

THANKSGIVING AFTER COMMUNION. From "ALL FOR JESUS." Price 1d. in wrapper.

A SCHEME OF INTERCESSORY PRAYER FOR THE MONTH. For the use of the Confraternity of the Precious Blood. Price 1d.

JESUS AND MARY, a Catholic Hymn Book. 1s.

THREE BEAUTIFUL PRINTS OF THE HOLY SOULS IN PURGATORY. With Verses. Price One Penny each.

THE LONDON ORATORY AND THE UNION NEWSPAPER. Being Three Letters on the Respect Due to Our Blessed Lord. 1d.

www.ingramcontent.com/pod-product-compliance
Lightning Source LLC
Chambersburg PA
CBHW022114160426
43197CB00009B/1018